NAUTICAL QUARTERLY

AUTUMN 1984

TABLE OF CONTENTS

PUBLISHER: DONALD C. McGRAW, JR.
EDITOR: JOSEPH GRIBBINS
DESIGNER: MARILYN ROSE
MANAGING EDITOR: MICHAEL LEVITT
ASSOCIATE EDITOR: REBECCA SMITH
DESIGN ASSISTANT: KAREN J. COOPER

MANAGING DIRECTOR: C.S. LOVELACE
CIRCULATION DIRECTOR: JOHN M. CORNWALL
CIRCULATION MANAGER: MATTHEW M. WITHERBEE
OFFICE MANAGER: LIZ MONTALVO
SPECIAL PROJECTS: LAURA RIEGEL
ASSISTANT TO THE PUBLISHER: deLANCEY FUNSTEN

ADVERTISING SALES REPRESENTATIVE:
MacDONALD FLANAGAN INC.
12 WEST 32nd STREET
9TH FLOOR
NEW YORK, N.Y. 10001
TELEPHONE 212-868-6220

CONTRIBUTING EDITORS:
H.D. "KNOTS" NESBITT/THE WEST COAST
ANGUS LENNOX/THE U.K.
ANNICA DAHLSTROM/SCANDINAVIA
MAXIM GOLIARD/THE CONTINENT
T. FREMANTLE FONG, JR./THE FAR EAST

THE LONELINESS OF A FINN SAILOR	MICHAEL LEVITT	3
THE GREAT OCEAN RACE OF 1866	JOHN ROUSMANIERE	20
NORMA JAY: WEST COAST IMPRESSIONS	REBECCA SMITH	28
HUCKINS—ALIVE AND WELL AT 56	STANLEY ROSENFELD	36
…AND NOT TO YIELD	TRISTAN JONES	54
YES, MR. LOOMIS, THERE ARE SOME SAILORS IN THE NAVY	FRASER FRASER-HARRIS	66
A DIVERSITY OF SEALS	RICHARD ELLIS	82
CENTURION 47—A SURVEY	FRASER FRASER-HARRIS	94
THE FIFES OF FAIRLIE	JOHN LEATHER	102
LETTERS		120
CREDITS		122

NAUTICAL QUARTERLY IS PUBLISHED IN WINTER, SPRING, SUMMER AND FALL BY NAUTICAL QUARTERLY CO., 373 PARK AVENUE SOUTH, NEW YORK, N.Y. 10016. COPYRIGHT © 1984 NAUTICAL QUARTERLY CO.; ALL RIGHTS RESERVED UNDER PAN AMERICAN AND UNIVERSAL COPYRIGHT CONVENTIONS; REPRODUCTION WITHOUT PERMISSION IS PROHIBITED. EDITORIAL SUBMISSIONS SHOULD BE SENT TO THE ADDRESS ABOVE, AND SHOULD BE ACCOMPANIED BY A SELF-ADDRESSED, STAMPED ENVELOPE. WE WILL ACCEPT NO RESPONSIBILITY, HOWEVER, FOR UNSOLICITED GRAPHIC OR EDITORIAL MATERIAL. ON EDITORIAL MATTERS, PHONE 212-685-9114. SUBSCRIPTION CORRESPONDENCE, BOOKSTORE ORDERS AND ORDERS FOR BACK COPIES SHOULD BE SENT TO THE ADDRESS ABOVE, OR BY PHONE TO 212-685-9114. U.S. SUBSCRIPTIONS ARE $60 PER YEAR. ALL OTHERS ARE $66 (U.S.). FOREIGN SUBSCRIBERS ARE SERVED ONLY BY SURFACE MAIL. SECOND-CLASS POSTAGE FOR NAUTICAL QUARTERLY (ISSN 0199-0837) IS PAID AT NEW YORK, N.Y. AND AT ADDITIONAL MAILING OFFICES. POSTMASTER: SEND ADDRESS CHANGES TO NAUTICAL QUARTERLY, DEPOT SQUARE, PETERBOROUGH, N.H. 03458.

THE LONELINESS OF A FINN SAILOR

BY MICHAEL LEVITT

NAUTICAL QUARTERLY

There would prove to be fierce competition in the Olympic trials in the Finn class in Long Beach, first on the race course and then in the protest room. The competition would take two weeks and the protest and maneuvering would take six. Coming in second in the Olympic trials is about as rewarding as coming in second in the America's Cup or in a boxing match. Only one entrant per country per class can sail in the Olympics, and two athletes, John Bertrand, in second place, and Russ Silvestri, in first, were locked in combat to make the United States team. ☐ These two Northern California competitors had raced against each other for years, and there seemed little love lost between them. They were a contrast in styles. Silvestri, 22, a recent business school graduate of USC, is big, blond, and brash. Bertrand is dark, on the small side for a Finn sailor, very self-contained and, at 28, something of a senior citizen for this most demanding singlehander. The very bearded Bertrand was by far the better-known; he had won the Finn Gold Cup in 1978 and two Laser World Championships in '76 and '77. In 1980, he made the U.S. Olympic team in the Finn, but found himself all dressed up with nowhere to go when President Carter elected not to send an Olympic team to Russia. In 1983, Bertrand worked as tactician to skipper John Kolius on *Courageous*, which sailed so brilliantly in the America's Cup defense trials. Most recently, Bertrand has been named tactician on the new 12-Meter *America II* that will represent the New York Yacht Club at the America's Cup in Perth, Australia, in 1987. ⚭

John Bertrand, left, talks with his coach, Bill Monti, on the morning before the last race of the Finn Olympic trials. Bertrand's comment to Monti was "Well, I have (Silvestri) where I want him. I'm in a position where I can win, so as long as I have that on the last day, that is all that I need."

Bertrand won the first Olympic trials race on April 28; Silvestri was second. Bertrand was third in the second race; Silvestri was fourth. "With my quick start," said Bertrand, "I started thinking Wow! The Olympic team! The opening ceremony! The free clothes! All that stuff that didn't have anything to do with winning the series." Then Russ Silvestri uncorked two strong races and Bertrand's thoughts turned to specifics. "Now I'm in second place, and I'm thinking things like Good start! Good rounding! And maybe Russ is thinking about the clothes, the opening ceremony, the press, the headlines."

On May 7th in an overheated Long Beach, the venue of 1984's Olympic sailing, only four-tenths of a point separated Bertrand from Silvestri after six races. The next day the Russians announced their boycott of the Olympics, citing security reasons. For Bertrand, the word from Moscow had a familiar ring to it. Bertrand would describe that sad sense of history repeating itself this way: "The Russian announcement happened during the seventh race. It was all over the radio, TV, and in the newspapers. It took the wind out of my sails a little bit. The feelings are still pretty close to the surface as far as '80 is concerned. There's no question about it, sports are politics, that's part of it; but, in truth, (the announcement) didn't make me feel particularly good."

The next day—predictably perhaps—Bertrand would finish over the rainbow in 12th place, and Silvestri would take a second. At the end of this race, Silvestri jumped overboard, a grand gesture of victory that lacked only the TV cameras and the Olympic theme. The wet grin on Russ Silvestri's face said that the contest was over. Silvestri was enjoying the spoils of victory, and his accessibility to the press increased. After Silvestri helped write his story for the morning papers, the reporters turned to Bertrand. He was asked: "How do you think Silvestri is going to do in the Olympics?" Bertrand, who rarely talks to the press in the heat of battle, said only that "I imagine he'll do pretty well; but, then again, it's not over yet."

Finn sailing is a lonely activity; before a racing series of this magnitude, competitors drift apart and keep their own counsel. It is a miserable boat to sail: slow—unlike the Laser to which it is often compared—and yet difficult if not impossible to keep flat. A premium is put on hiking for hours on end, and the typically beefy Finn sailor augments his weight by wearing 30 pounds of water bottles. This awkward 15′ dinghy is a chiropractor's or knee-surgeon's dream. Despite its macho image, the boat has a low-tech look, like something that was designed in 1949, which it was. "The aim of the Finn designer," wrote British journalist A. C. Pye, "was to produce a boat that would torture its helmsman to the limit of human endurance, while at the same time testing his self-control to the utmost with unusual profusions of unusual gear."

When John Bertrand sails a Finn, he turns inward. Asked if he enjoys the boat, Bertrand said, "I enjoy the demands of the boat, and I sort of enjoy the mystique about it, about the physical and emotional demands it makes." To the question: Is Finn sailing lonely? Bertrand said, "I find it enjoyable, actually. It gives me an opportunity to collect my thoughts. You're in total control of your destiny."

There is another reason that Bertrand looks within during competition. He told this story: "A reporter from the Los Angeles Times came up to me before this series when I first got to the beach, and was unpacking my boat. He said, 'John Bertrand, I'd love to do an article about you; it has to do with the boycott in '80.' I stopped him there and said, 'I don't talk to the press during a series. I understand you guys have got to make a living; I'm really sympathetic; but it's too distracting.' He started arguing, but I said, 'You write a story, and maybe it says I'm supposed to win. I then have to worry about how it affects my competitors. I have to think about how it affects me.' I said no way."

Then Bertrand spoke about Silvestri, "I think Russ is a little immature. He didn't have the patience to hold it in. You have to be a good winner. You can't rub your competitors' noses in it. You've got to get self-satisfaction from it. Russ' satisfaction seems to be public. I think that can have a damaging effect."

On May 10th, Bertrand returned from the dead by maintaining second place on each of the nine legs; at one point in this race Silvestri was as far back as 10th. But Silvestri is quick, and methodically and with a poker-player's cool he clawed his way back into the race and finished third. Race ten would decide the Olympic question in the Finn Class. Bertrand had to win, and if he did Silvestri could finish no lower than third.

Russ Silvestri gave a strange interview on the eve of this contest. He told Don Borst of the Long Beach Press-Telegram, that, "I just hope (Bertrand) doesn't win, and I'm going to do everything I can to keep that (Bertrand winning) from happening." Later he added, "If I have to go over the (starting) line early to stay with him, I will. I can't let him get away from me like I did today."

The greatness John Bertrand unquestionably has has not come easily. The likes of John Bertrand—these dinghy hotshots who grew up in that most physical of boats, the Laser—have turned sailing on this level into a game of highly trained athletes. Before they came along, dinghy racing was mostly a game of sportsmen, who were more likely to bench press a beer than a barbell. From two ballet classes a day, to pumping iron three times a day, to days, weeks, months, and years of training (not sitting) in a sailboat, Bertrand comes prepared to win. He will use what he has to beat you, and that includes the rules.

Bertrand read what Silvestri said in the newspaper. He knew the tactic of premature starting and how potent a weapon it is. He had, in fact, used it himself. On the morning of the race, Bertrand called a friend in San Francisco, someone he knew from the St. Francis Yacht Club. The friend was Tom Blackaller, who knows a lot about winning sailboat races and who is usually willing to talk about it. Blackaller's comment was to the point: "Bertrand, you're screwed!" he said. Bertrand described the conversation this way: "Tom said he'd been in that situation before, and there is nothing you can do to defend against it. He also stressed that he thinks (this tactic) is one thing that is totally wrong with our sport. The last race of a series should always count. Tom feels pretty strongly about that, and he's been voicing that opinion for years. That got me thinking, and I re-read the rules. Under the fair-sailing rule it says that a yacht may be disqualified...only in the case of a clear-cut violation of certain principles, which are fair sailing, superior speed, and skill."

On this page is Russ Silvestri, of Tiburon, Calif. Silvestri, age 22, a recent graduate of USC, is eminently fast in this Olympic singlehander, but the 1984 Olympic trials would prove that the race isn't always to the swift. The competition in this series would come down to Silvestri, in Finn 1074, and John Bertrand, in Finn 1050. Silvestri's controversial tactics in the last race—in which he started prematurely and "harassed" John Bertrand—may have brought his ouster from the regatta, under rule 75.2 ("after a gross breach of good manners or sportsmanship, the race committee may exclude a competitor either from further participation in a series or from the whole series, or take some disciplinary action."). On the right-hand page are several portraits of John Bertrand. Finn 1073, to leeward of Bertrand in the top-left photo, was sailed by Buzz Reynolds, who was the Olympic selection while appeals were pending.

The America's Cup saw Bertrand's appreciation for the rules grow, as did his facility to use them. He said, "I used to sail—I won two Laser World Championships, numerous national and North American Championships—and I didn't know anything about the rules. I knew port-starboard. My knowledge of the rules at that time was what I had experienced on the race course. I'd come to a mark and say, 'You can't do that,' but I wouldn't know why. I wouldn't know the appeals. I was very naïve, probably until last summer in Newport, when I came in contact with the people who wrote the rules. The rules have a lot of gray areas to

> "*I* STARTED THINKING, THE OLYMPIC TEAM! THE OPENING CEREMONY! THE FREE CLOTHES!"

them. You have to know the spirit of the rules, why they were written. When I was with *Courageous*, I spent many long hours reading the Appeals Book. It is really important to know that stuff."

Bertrand wanted a second opinion about Silvestri's possible tactic, so he called Tom F. Ehman, Jr., executive director of the United States Yacht Racing Union (USYRU) in Newport, R.I. Bertrand mentioned the Silvestri quote in the paper. According to Bertrand, Ehman, who likewise was familiar with the tactic, said that he would look very negatively on such an attempt to interfere with fair sailing. Ehman recommended that he take the newspaper article to the international jury. This Bertrand did, before the race. He also approached Silvestri. "I went up to Russ and said, 'Have you read the fair sailing rule?' He kind of nodded acknowledgment, and I said, 'If you start early you can plan on seeing my protest flag.' His response was something like, Oh yeah, tough guy." Bertrand was asked why he alerted Silvestri. "I wanted to let him know that something was up. I didn't want this to be a complete surprise to him, and the second thing was that I wanted him to start behind the line to give me a chance to get away so I could win the race."

On May 11, in light winds and in a sloppy ground swell, 28 Finn sailors, representing this country's best singlehanders, started their 10-minute war dance. Race 10 would settle the Olympic question. Twice during the countdown, Finn 1074, sailed by Russ Silvestri of Tiburon, Calif., and Finn 1050, sailed by John Bertrand, of Anaheim Hills, Calif., engaged each other in 12-Meter fashion, and both times Bertrand seemed to get the better of the circling. Then, with 25 seconds remaining in the last race of the 1984 Olympic trials, Silvestri crossed the starting line early. The gun sounded, and then came a second shot, signaling a premature starter. Silvestri—as the newspaper said he would—started early and then camped on his rival's wind with a tenacity that could suffocate a lesser man.

Bertrand described the action on the race course. "I got around him on the first leg by false-tacking him, but he is so damn fast in the light and sloppy stuff, or else I'm so slow, he just started wiggling the tiller a little bit and came back. He got in front of me again before the weather mark. At one point in the race we were out to the left of the fleet, kind of reaching in a little bit, and I said to Russ, 'It looks like we've caught up to these guys.' He started laughing and relaxed a little bit. I said, 'Russ, did the jury talk to you before you left the beach?' He said 'no,' so I added, 'Well, I talked to the jury this morning and they are *real* interested in what's going on here right now!' I could see the color drain from his face. Prior to that he was doing a good job of holding me back, and then all of a sudden I could see it working on him. He wasn't as aggressive."

They crossed the finish line, Bertrand in ninth place, Silvestri ranked as a premature starter. Bertrand held up a red protest flag. With Bertrand's abysmal performance this day, Buzz Reynolds, of Summit, New Jersey, moved into second place overall. Bertrand finished third in the series. It would take the sport's governing body many weeks to work its way through this mess.

John Bertrand is the complete sailor. He has been training for greatness in his sport since he was six years old. Bertrand was born in San Mateo, south of San Francisco, as the youngest of seven children. "My father joined the Palo Alto Yacht Club to get us out of the house on weekends, so we wouldn't drive my mom nuts," said Bertrand. "It didn't work—she's still crazy." His first boat was an El Toro, which he sailed on a lagoon near Foster City, the tract community where he lived, a place blessed with numerous waterways and good (if shifty) wind. Bertrand was raised by his father, a man who made and lost fortunes at various times.

In 1970, a man visited San Rafael High School and asked the assistant principal if the school might be interested in a sailing program. The principal summoned Bill Monti, the recently appointed head of the school's physical education program. Monti described the meeting: "He offered us a sailing program because he and his wife had separated. He had a couple of sons living with him, one of whom would eventually be attending school here, and he wanted this kid exposed to a yacht-club environment. His reasoning was that yacht-club people are good people. They have high values, high moral standards, and they are family-type people. That is the environment he wanted his son to know. But, as a single parent, he wasn't going to have the time to be with the kid as much as he wanted. He wanted to pave the way for him and make sure he was taken care of, and exposed to a good environment."

Monti allowed that they had no resources for such a program. The man said, "I have a friend who has a dock across the street from the high school, and he'll let you use it. He also has a Banshee; you can use that, too. I have a couple of friends who are also interested in seeing this type of program created, and they will be happy to lend you boats. I'll also write up a syllabus. I will also provide you with my son who is a terrific sailor, and he can be a teacher's aide, or something. If there are any technical questions, he'll be able to answer them."

Although Monti knew little about sailing, he was enthusiastic about the offer. "I mean, how often do you have something like that offered to you?" Nevertheless, he realized that classes had already been scheduled for the next year. He welcomed the offer but said it would be impossible to organize until the following year. "The man's response was, 'No! It had to be right now.' At this point he told us that his son John was an incoming freshman. We said we'd do it. We'd take a swimming class or some other water-related activity and make sailing an elective."

Monti continued: "Well, as promised, the boats materialized, the site materialized, and John appeared on the scene with his smiling face. He was a shy, timid young man, who seemingly had gone unnoticed by 99% of his teachers and peers. He was very shy, probably because he was left alone excessively. He was the youngest of seven children."

John Bertrand was 14 when he entered high school. He was 5'4" tall, and weighed 98 pounds on a good day. His size, remembered Monti, belied his competitiveness when sailing. "He was feisty in a sailboat. In our classes, we'd do drills, and if someone got ahead of him, he'd capsize them rather than let them go. Even then there was just no second for John. He liked to be in front. I thought of him as an incredibly good sailor back then. He had this tenacity—a quality that is so necessary in any great competitor. You see, my background is not sailing. I coached football, basketball, soccer and track...But I could see that John had the capacity to be a good sailor; I say 'good' because I didn't know what a great sailor was."

Bertrand sailed 13' Banshees—a boat that in some ways was a forerunner of the Laser—with much success. In fact, he won the Banshee National Championship in 1972 and 1973. He also joined the junior sailing program of the St. Francis Yacht Club. He tried out for and made the club's junior sailing team in 1973. Said Bertrand, "The club had just purchased several Lasers. They made them available to the juniors. They had a great old truck then—an F100 or something, built in '56 or thereabouts. It had a flat bed, and it was all dented up. It was just great. The yacht club gave us the truck and a trailer, and a credit card and said, 'You want to go to the Santa Cruz Open or the North Americans? Go!'"

At the St. Francis Yacht Club Bertrand first met Tom Blackaller, sailmaker and sailor extraordinaire. Blackaller won his first of two Star World Championships in 1974. "Tom was a real friendly guy," remembered Bertrand. "I introduced myself one day and said, 'Tom, can I ask you a question? I'm going to the Laser Worlds in Germany, and I don't really have much experience. Is there anything you can tell me that would help me?' He bought me a coke, and he told me all about sailing in Europe, about the wind conditions, and how they compare to what we have in San Francisco Bay. And then he went on and explained all the different nuances of sailing in Europe and how to sail in a big world championship fleet. At the end of the conversation I was walking ten feet in the air." Bertrand would win that Laser World Championship in 1976 and again the next year.

Even in high school, sailing was his life. In his senior year Bertrand approached Bill Monti for some extra tutoring. Monti described it this way: "John came to me. He said, 'Bill, what I really need is someone to coach me in getting physically fit.' That is what he was after. He knew that I really couldn't help him with his sailing. Having tried to teach sailing, I recognized that sailing is a very complex sport. There are probably more variables that are less constant than in any other activity. As a result of that, I could see that helping John had to be handled in a special way. I said, 'John, you're the sailor, but I'll handle the fitness part.' What we included in the fitness part was endurance, range of motion, strength, and mental preparation. In that context emerged a lot of things, but mostly we were friends. I have to tell you that my wife literally went crazy when John came over, because she said that when we were together it was almost like the rest of the world was tuned out. We'd talk for hours."

During last summer's America's Cup, Bertrand described the special relationship he has to this day with Monti. "We'd talk about races. I'd come back from a weekend of racing, and I'd tell him that I'd won. He'd say, 'Well, why did you win?' After a while I'd come back from a race, and I'd say to Bill, 'Well, I had this problem.' And he, being a very observant fellow, would say, 'Well, didn't you tell me last year that you were doing this and this? Why don't you try that.'

"I went to the Laser Worlds in Germany in 1976, and I won. I came back almost discouraged because I felt I could have done much better. I was surprised I was able to win. In talking to Bill about it, he brought up the question: What if you really get good, where does it end? At that point I asked him if he would help me get to the Olympics. From that point on, he officially became my coach."

Bertrand would begin his day by running five or six miles. Then there would be weight lifting, sometimes as often as three times a day. And there would also be sail training; but Bertrand and his coach did it in a special way. In these days of sports psychology and advanced coaching techniques, perhaps some of this seems familiar, but Monti and Bertrand were making it up as they went along and applying it to a sport in which it had never been tried before. Monti described the sailing technique this way. "We used something we called visualization. What we would do is close our eyes, and imagine, if you will, a situation. We'd put two boats together in our minds. And say we're going to practice a given situation. Maybe shadow someone. You know how bloody difficult it is to put two boats together in such a drill. In real life it can take half the day before you get any meaningful practice. Well John would practice alone, and people were always mystified how he could practice alone, but he was never really alone. He had what we called the 'phantom' along. He was always practicing with the phantom."

He continued on this theme: "A lot of people go out and sail. It said in this morning's paper how Russ (Silvestri) has only missed five days of

> "*IF I HAVE TO GO OVER THE LINE EARLY, I WILL. I CAN'T LET (BERTRAND) GET AWAY FROM ME LIKE TODAY.*"

sailing in the last 300. And this is meant as no criticism of Russ because I don't know what he did, but I say: how good was it? To be sitting in a boat—we call that seat time. It may not, in fact, have been any value at all. It may have proven how good a loafer someone is. We did this mental thing that meant that every minute we were out on the water John was working on something that actually had a direct and usable function in a race. We didn't have to wait for another boat to come and catch up with him, or get on the starboard side in position. John would go out for an hour or two with the phantom and have really an hour or two of meaningful practice."

One day Bertrand complained to Monti about his body movement. "I'm really clumsy on a boat," he told him. Monti suggested gymnastics or, perhaps, ballet. "I told him 'If you're concerned about your ego, gymnastics would be the one for you, but if you can handle it, then to my mind it's dance.' One of the things we thought was important was to pay the price. I constantly said to John, 'You've got to be in the best physical condition,' and we worked on that. I also said, 'you've got to be mentally fitter. It will take a lot of guts to do dance, but going the distance might

*H*E WORE LEOTARDS "USUALLY UNDER SWEATS," HE SAID, "BUT IT WAS NO BIG DEAL."

also make a big difference in your mental fitness.'"

Bertrand enrolled in a ballet class. Asked his feelings when he walked in the door for the first session, he said, "I was scared shitless." So, in addition to running five or six miles each morning, lifting weights three times a day, and sailing with the phantom for two hours of "meaningful practice," Bertrand took two and sometimes three dance classes each evening. He wore leotards "usually under sweats," he said, "but it was no big deal." The ballet teacher was receptive and quite supportive to Bertrand's dance career. And since there was never much money, she gave him scholarships. Monti commented that John got quite good at dance. "John does a pretty good leap and twirl," he said.

Bertrand was asked if the dance proved helpful to his sailing? He said, "Absolutely! First I got stronger, all over, my legs and upper body. Also I really got stretched out. The most important lesson I learned was how to work my body...It gave me knowledge of how to work the body more efficiently." Monti, however, saw the gains more in terms of psychological payments. As he said, "The ballet helped enormously in terms of self confidence. He was the one sucking it up out there. He knew he had paid the price, had gone the extra step..."

Bertrand and Monti set goals on an annual basis. Monti described the sessions this way: "I have some background in movement education, and one tenet in movement education is that you have to be successful. So we'd set goals, but the goals weren't necessarily that you have to win, maybe it was something like you are to do well in two of three regattas. One thing we learned is that John could always finish third or better in any regatta. Always. So when he got in trouble, I'd say 'relax, you can take the day off and get a third.' From that we learned how important it was to relax. I never gave John a goal he couldn't achieve. In fact, he almost always surpassed the goals we set."

They never let money, or lack thereof, interfere with the pursuit of these goals. Recalled Monti: "We set our goals for the entire year. We'd name regattas that he was to go do and how he was to do, and it didn't matter where in the world they were. We didn't know where the money would come from. I'd say to John, 'You know, if you're going to be a world champion for the second time in the Laser, you've got to go to this competition and that competition. He'd look at me with that shy puppy dog look, but he'd never ask how. Now there were times when his father had money, and he paid. Other times people came out of the woodwork, and sometimes it was by the seat of his pants, and it was lucky he got there, but rarely did he miss a commitment.

"We had to build something of a revenue-producing capability into our system. For example, when he went on to win his second world championship in the Laser, the real goal was the Olympics and the Finn, and to that end he had to meet people in the Finn Class, who could make boats available to him and with whom he could live. So making friends was part of the program. It was often the only way he was going to be able to take advantage of an opportunity to get out and sail. To get the experience. And with John's shyness, that wasn't always the easiest part of the program."

The goal in 1980 was to win the gold medal in the Finn class in the Olympics. "Anything before that didn't matter," said Bertrand. The Finn Gold Cup—the world championship in this class—was in January in New Zealand. Before Bertrand left for this competition, news of our Olympic boycott was in the air. "You couldn't really let it affect you. It wasn't real; it was political stuff," Bertrand said. Midway through the competition in New Zealand, the official word came. "All of a sudden we're boycotting," said Bertrand, "and my first thought was I've got to win the world championship."

Bertrand was in second place at the time to another American, the ever-swift Cam Lewis. Bertrand could win his second Finn Gold Cup if he could keep Lewis below 12th place, a tall order to be sure. And it was blowing, the very conditions in which Lewis is at his best. Bertrand described the last race: "So my tactic was to match-race him before the start and prevent him from getting a good start. I almost did it, but he rubbed me off on another boat and just got away. He got a great start, and I started behind the fleet. But the amazing thing was that I worked my way back to him. It was blowing 30 knots; it was one of the windiest series I've ever sailed. I was taking so many chances downwind, and when you take a chance in a Finn downwind when it is blowing that hard, you are either making big gains or you're swimming.

"We virtually rounded the weather mark within two boat lengths. On the last run before the last beat, it was real puffy. Lewis started to go out of control, so he's sailing a higher course to the left. I kept it under control—actually sailing by the lee and heading straight for the mark. So he's going to have to make two jibes to make the mark. I have to make one, but there's a third boat in there—Chris Law from England—on my starboard side, on port tack. I'm on starboard, Law goes out of control, and we're converging at a very rapid rate; there's no way that I can whip off a jibe in those conditions. What I have to do is shove it over as hard as I can. I almost shot head to wind, and then I just jerked it down as hard as I could, and the boat went into a death roll so far that I'm still surprised today that I didn't flip over. The rudder is out of the water—there's a picture of it—and then—boom—I rounded right back up into the wind after the death roll, jerked it off again, and whipped in a jibe. The mark was coming up; Lewis was converging; he had an inside overlap; we rounded the mark

overlapped, and he just whaled on me upwind in a tacking duel. Those were great races that we had."

The Olympic trials were held in May in Newport, R.I., and for Bertrand, who had spent three years training in this most solitary and most miserable of boats, they were important to win, lack of the Olympics notwithstanding. Bertrand said, "I knew it was pretty important to win the trials. I don't think that everybody felt that way—Cam by this time had lost interest—but I knew it was important for me."

Monti wrote him a letter just before the trials. "I talked about

LIKE MANY OLYMPIC ATHLETES, BERTRAND FOUND THE SUMMER OF 1980 UNSATISFYING. UNFINISHED.

democracy," he related, "and the fact that we are a free country. We have an opportunity here to make choices, and that we stood up to the world as a model. I also said that the political consequences of an invasion (the Russian invasion of Afghanistan—Carter's reason for the Olympic boycott) probably wouldn't make a whole lot of difference to John Bertrand, but a lot of people were looking at John Bertrand. It was important that despite what a government official might do, that athletes like John be willing to stand behind it, right or wrong." Bertrand, then age 24 and seemingly at the peak of his powers and ability, won the Olympic trials. He was considered a shoo-in for the gold medal had the U.S. gone to Russia.

Sam Merrick, head of the U.S. Olympic Yachting Committe, helped set up an alternate sailing competition in Germany. Said Bertrand: "By the time I got there, I realized I couldn't do it. I was just totally burned out. I told Sam how I felt, but he said that it's really important that I give it a try. I realized that Sam kind of went out on a limb to stage this competition, so I decided to give it my best shot. I got out there and had nothing to give. In the second race it came to a head. I got a bad start, and I'm sailing slow on the beat. My sail was all worn out; I hadn't bought any new sails since the boycott. I decided this is crazy. If it were a different boat that was fun to sail, I probably could have gotten through it, but the boat just demands so much. I quit."

After 20 years in dinghies, Bertrand found himself more or less on the beach. He took a job in Alameda. Then, in 1982, John Kolius, who had just been named skipper of *Courageous*, called. "When Kolius called, he said that there's a slot open as tactician. 'Do you think you might be interested in coming down?' Kolius is really low-key; I talked to him a couple of times about this, but we kept our distance. Finally, I said to him, 'What's your motivation for all of this?' He said, 'I'm just here to help Tom (Blackaller) beat *Liberty*, and then we'll see what we can do against Tom.' So I said, 'I'll tell you what, if you're there to help Tom win the America's Cup, I'm not interested, but if you want to win the America's Cup, then we're talking.'"

And *Courageous* talked quite eloquently, easily handling her stablemate *Defender*, sailed by Tom Blackaller, and taking Dennis Conner and *Liberty* down to the wire. As a loner suddenly thrust into a position of leadership over a madding crowd of 12-Meter sailors, Bertrand found the summer very rewarding. As he said, "It was great. I enjoyed the team aspect of it all. You might say that I was a bit of a snob when I first came to it. I always felt that the individual effort was the supreme effort; but, then again, I always wondered what it would be like to be on a football team, you know a pulling guard or something. One of many.

"I felt that what I did on the 12 Meter was to pump up the crew. We did our best when we were totally out of control. When we were screaming and yelling and the jib was just barely getting in. I think it was just the fiber of our crew. You know when we tried to be really calm and controlled, I think we became too passive. Maybe we didn't have that capacity, maybe it wasn't our style. But out of control, that's when we did our best."

Like many Olympic athletes, Bertrand found the summer of 1980 unsatisfying. Unfinished. He was haunted by thoughts of what might have been. He would be 28 when the Olympic flame burned again, and that is old for a Finn sailor. When we talked during the America's Cup, he seemed finished with this most demanding little boat. Asked why the decision to sail again, Bertrand said, "I made the decision to do it because the boat was sitting in my backyard. I had spent so much time and money over the years training for the Olympics, I probably would have regretted it for the rest of my life if I didn't make a stab at it.

"Actually I found getting back into the boat easy. The 12-Meter program was great for my Finn sailing because it came at a low period for me. The worst thing about the boycott was that it was so unexpected. If I could have plugged that in as a variable, then maybe I would have handled it better. The 12 Meter got me psyched up for sailing again, plus it increased my knowledge of the sport. I was psyched about getting back into the boat. I was surprised how quickly the technique came back. I started moving and doing things in the Finn without thinking about them. I'm older and maybe it has gotten easier. Before I always considered myself small for the boat. I'd get to a point where I would crumble. Physically I was ruined, but now I've put on 15 pounds—I now weigh 190—and it seems like I can handle the loads better."

On the eve of the last Olympic trials race, Bertrand broke training. "The night before, I went out to dinner with my friend Steve Black, his wife, and another sailor. I was incredibly happy. I wanted it to come down to the last race, if nothing else. To win that last race was going to be an incredible challenge, and I was psyched. I had four drinks; I forgot all about my training—you know, eating carbos and stuff like that. That day, I had picked out a wedding ring for Andrea, my fiancée. During the race the next day I wore it around my neck. That was symbolic for me because Andrea has been such a big part of this effort, and obviously a very big part of my life. Everyone that I'm in contact with affects what I do, and I try to bring them into what I do."

John's coach and friend, Bill Monti, came down from San Francisco to watch him race that last day, something Monti rarely does, as he is not, he emphasizes, an on-the-water coach. He had a few quiet moments with John before this most important contest. Asked what he said, Monti commented, "I told John that I didn't come down to watch him sail, I came down to watch him win. And he knew that's why I came. Maybe I was saying it for my own frailties, if you will, maybe as a lack of knowing the right thing to say, but invariably the right thing to say is what comes from the heart, so we say it. John's comment was, 'Well, I have him right where I want him. I'm in a position where I can win, so as long as I have that on the last day, that is all that I need.'"

It was not to be this day, on the race course. With Bertrand's ninth-place finish, Buzz Reynolds moved ahead of him into second place. Bertrand, in Finn 1050, was first to hit the beach after the lonely hour's sail from the race course. He was greeted by the press, whom he politely ignored, and by his fiancée, Andrea Adame. They embraced—they hadn't seen each other in weeks—and then Bertrand retrieved his Finn from the water. Also waiting for him were Bill Monti and John's father. Bertrand seemed delighted to see them, but purposefulness was written on his face. Ahead of John Bertrand was a very important protest meeting. On the way to the hearing, he encountered Buzz Reynolds. "I wouldn't leave if I were you," Bertrand said. According to Bertrand, Reynolds said he wasn't interested in going to the Olympics as a result of a protest.

Pipeline is the magazine of the U.S. Olympic Yachting Committee. In the issue that was circulating at the Olympic trials there is an article by Bill Ficker, who defended the America's Cup in 1970. Ficker is a senior judge of the USYRU, and in this capacity he has served as the jury for the Congressional Cup, among other contests. Ficker wrote about the use of rules: "It always seems incredible to me that so many world-class sailors give so much attention to boat speed, crew training, and development of state-of-the-art equipment, and almost totally ignore an equally significant part of their campaign: learning the rules. The rules are the foil in the art of fencing with sailboats, and without the sharpest foil and the understanding of how to use it, you are jeopardizing your entire effort, or at least compromising it...Competitor enforcement of the rules is the tradition in our sport, and when the rules are not followed we owe it to ourselves and our fellow competitors, for the quality of the racing, to protest."

Bertrand protested Silvestri under the fundamental rule—fair sailing—and Rule 75.2, penalties for gross infringement of rules or misconduct. The rulemakers believe that gross infringement is an egregious offense, and the penalty for the above (reads Case 78) is that a yacht can be "excluded from the whole series, and all her results shall be struck from the records as if she had not started in any of the races." Also to loom large at the protest hearing was the Press-Telegraph article in which Silvestri discussed his tactic.

The competitors presented their cases. Then the international jury deliberated for two and a half hours. Late that Friday night the verdict came in. Silvestri was out of the Olympic trials. There were angry words exchanged in the night.

Finn sailing is a lonely pastime. So is protesting a yacht, whether the contest is a Wednesday night beer-can race or the Olympic trials. Asked if it was a hard decision to make, Bertrand replied, "I owe it to the people who have supported me. I owe it to my family to do the best I can do. I'm not one who is going to sit by and let something pass that I feel strongly about. So I did it. I don't think a lot of people would. I have my standards, so I felt strongly about it, and if people don't approve, it doesn't bother me a bit."

Postscript: The question of who would be the Finn representative burned for weeks. As I write this, 47 days after the trials were held, there is still no clearcut answer to that question, although not for want of trying: the Olympic representative has changed five times in those seven weeks. For those who care about such things, this tangled skein of protest, appeal, and litigation could profoundly affect the sport.

The protest hearing between Bertrand and Silvestri occurred on May 11, the night of the last race. The jury found these facts: "...(Finn) 1074 (Silvestri) crossed the line 20 to 25 seconds before the starting signal on starboard (and) proceeded 20-30 feet beyond the line and tacked to port. She then reached parallel to the line (for about 20 seconds) until the starting signal...

"The race committee properly made the recall signals and 1074 made no attempt to return to start properly.

"Three experienced race officers, including one extraordinarily experienced race officer, testified that it would have been impossible for any experienced racer not to have known that he was a premature starter.

"Over the length of the course and at every apparent opportunity 1074 slowed, blocked and harassed 1050 (Bertrand) both by depriving her of clear air and by slowing to disturb her air.

"The skipper of 1074, prior to the race and to at least two people, stated that he intended, if he thought it necessary to start prematurely to gain an advantage to permit him to keep 1050 from winning, he would do it. During the hearing, the skipper of 1074 denied several times even the substance of these remarks, some of which had been published."

Then the committee announced its decision and the grounds for making it: "1074 was deliberately a premature starter in order to gain an unfair advantage. This put her in a position to slow, block and harass 1050, which she did at every apparent opportunity throughout the race. 1074 deliberately infringed IYRR (International Yacht Racing Rule) 51.1(b) ('Unless otherwise prescribed in the sailing instructions, a yacht which either crosses prematurely, or is on the course side of the starting line, or its extensions, at the starting signal, shall return and start in accordance with the definition.') by failing to return to start correctly...

"The combination of the deliberate infringement of the rules and the flagrant violation of the Fundamental Rule—Fair Sailing—constitutes a gross breach of sportsmanship.

"In addition, the Jury is satisfied that the skipper of 1074 did, on more than one occasion during the hearing, fail to tell the truth.

"1074 is removed from the series and is to be scored as if she did not compete in any race under the provision of IYRR 75.2 ('after a gross breach of good manners or sportsmanship the race committee may exclude a competitor either from further participation in a series or from the whole series or take other disciplinary action.')."

Then Bertrand petitioned the jury for redress, which was heard on May 13. The initial petition was denied—primarily because Bertrand hadn't had sufficient time to prepare his case—but the door was left ajar for another presentation. He tried again the next day, and the hearing was reopened. By conference call, the jury heard Bertrand's contention under Rule 69(c) that he should be granted redress. The salient part of the rule reads: "A yacht which alleges that her finishing position has been materially prejudiced through no fault of her own by...being disabled by another vessel which was required to keep clear, may request redress from the protest committee..."

Without rendering a decision, the jury queried the Appeals Committee of USYRU. They wanted a definition of the word "disabled." The jury wanted to know if Bertrand was "disabled" by Silvestri if no collision or no damage occurred. Rule 69(c) is a hard one to win; the Appeals Committee's response was to the point. "No," they said, meaning Bertrand was not *disabled* by Silvestri.

Then the jury considered redress under Rule 69(a); that is, "A yacht which alleges that her finishing position has been materially prejudiced through no fault of her own by...an action or omission of the race committee" may be entitled to redress. The jury concluded that the race committee should have canceled the race in view of Silvestri's action. Under Rule 5.1(b), the race committee can abandon a race after it has started "...for reasons directly affecting...the fairness of the competition."

The jury wrote in explanation on May 28: "In establishing as equitable an arrangement as possible for all yachts concerned...the jury orders that Finn 1050 (Bertrand) be scored as specified in IYRR Appendix 5 (Olympic scoring system).

"That is...equal to the average points...that she had received in all previous races of the series. And that the point scores of all other yachts in the race are to remain as last previously scored.

"...The jury is satisfied, that is, aware, of the relevant facts and of the probable consequences of its action in granting the redress to Finn 1050, including those relating to (Finn) 1073, Buzz Reynolds, which was previously scored as winning the event. For Finn 1073, in contrast to Finn 1050, immediately prior to Race 10, had no mathematical chance, unless Finn 1074's results were expunged from the series, of winning the Finn Class Olympic trials.

"Accordingly, the jury considers the decision more equitable than the decision which it reached prior to reopening the hearing."

The jury that rendered this decision, on May 28, was composed of six prominent men in the sport in this country, among them was Chuck Kober, USYRU president. They would not have the last word, however, despite this notice in the sailing instructions: "a jury appointed by USYRU shall be the final arbiter of all other protests under the ... rules."

Silvestri immediately filed an appeal and grievance. Then one day later, the allegedly reluctant James "Buzz" Reynolds also filed one. Three men made up the Review Board that adjudicated this matter: Noel M. Field, Jr. was chairman, while the two other members were William Ficker, and William Dalessi.

The Review Board heard it as an appeal, under Article 14, section 3 (b). (Note the word *appeal*, that will become important to our story.) The main question under discussion during this hearing was, whether Silvestri's action "was a 'gross' breach of the applicable standard?"

It is interesting to note that looming largely at this hearing was the fact that Bertrand had used the same tactic at the 1980 Finn Nationals. (There was no protest filed in that case.) Also under discussion, was Case 78, involving two yachts in the Flipper class. This case, which occurred in

1975, closely—if not exactly—paralleled what happened in the Finn trials. There the premature starter was removed from the series.

The majority ruled on June 12 that Silvestri's action did not constitute "gross infringement"; that this tactic "was commonly accepted within the Finn fleet," and that there were "substantial factual differences" between what happened here and Case 78. They also considered important the fact that "Silvestri had no knowledge of Case 78..."

The decision was not unanimous, however. Dissenting was Chairman Noel M. Field, Jr. In his dissenting opinion, Field wrote "Acceptance by the Finn Class or by certain leaders of that Class does not make the tactic acceptable to the USYRU..." Also, the chairman saw a direct parallel between what happened in Long Beach and Case 78. In any event the majority ruled, and Silvestri was back in the Olympics.

John Bertrand appealed that decision to the Executive Committee of the USYRU, which met on June 22. It was an august body, chaired by William Lynn, a vice-president of the USYRU. If the matter was complex, the decision was simple: the Executive Committee ruled the three-man Appeals Committee had no authority to hear this case as an appeal. "The right of appeal was properly denied in the notice of race and the sailing instructions," they wrote. That reinstated the May 28th decision of the jury, making Bertrand the Olympic representative.

Furthermore, the Executive Committee offered this opinion of matters: "In the process of arriving at its decision, (this committee) has reviewed the entire record in detail, including all materials and testimony submitted by and on behalf of R. Silvestri, and has found no basis to support a grievance against the jury in the light of IYRU Case 78."

Silvestri has these choices: he can ask the Review Board to hear the matter as a grievance; he can petition the United States Olympic Committee to settle the matter under Article 14; he can appeal the decision to the American Arbitration Association, or he can drop the matter.

THE GREAT OCEAN

BY JOHN ROUSMANIERE

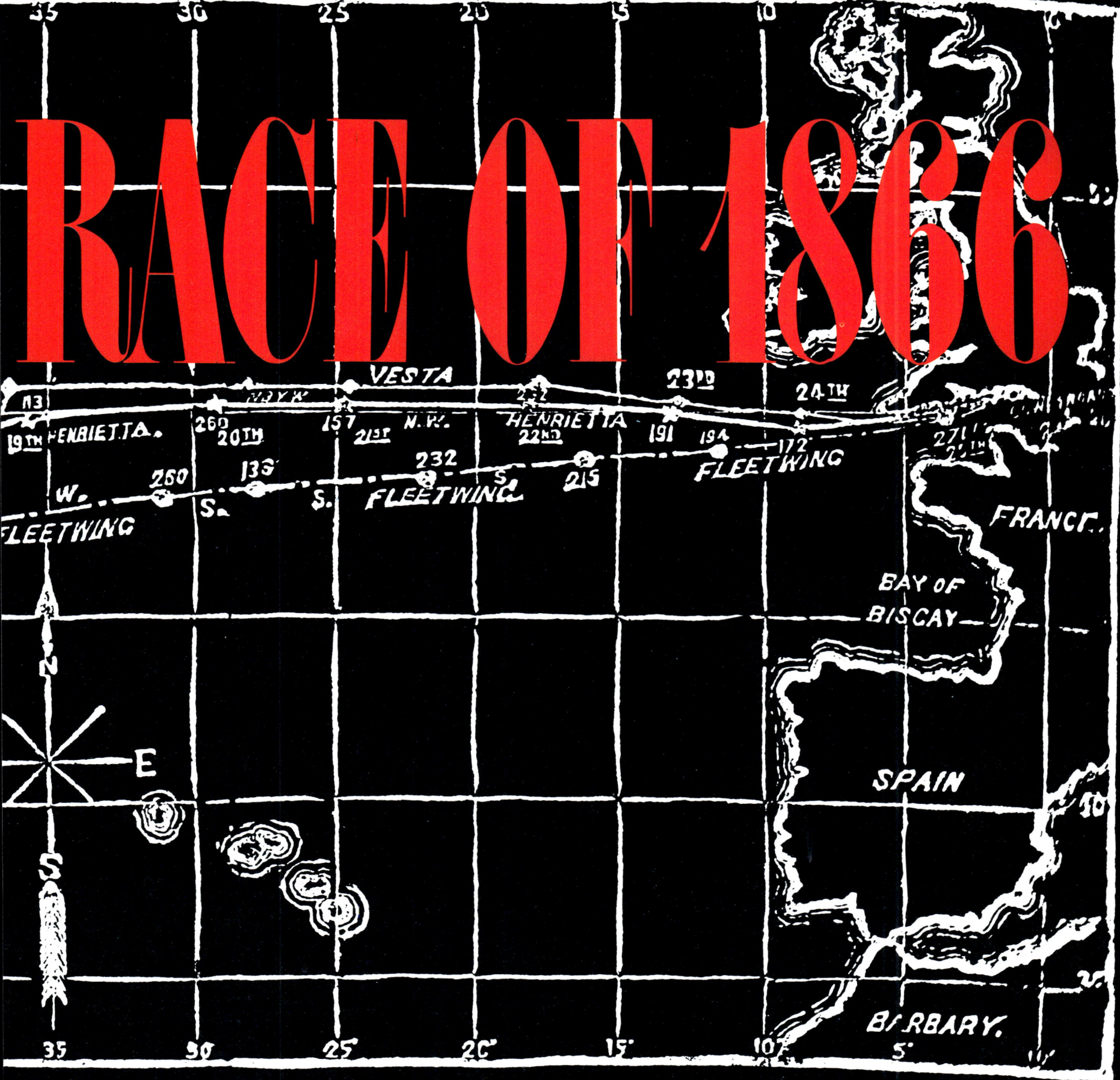

Fifteen years after *America's* astonishing and, for John Cox Stevens and his syndicate brothers, profitable visit to Cowes in 1851, another three 100′ American schooners sailed across the Atlantic in a race that would have left Stevens gasping in disbelief. Of all the events in the history of yachting, none is stranger than the first long ocean race. A breakneck sprint from New York to the Isle of Wight for stakes of $90,000, it was sailed in the unpropitious month of December and resulted in the sport's first major disaster. □ For years an event of such sheer craziness had been building as the wheeler-dealer tycoons of the New York Yacht Club built ever-bigger schooners to race ever-longer distances up and down the Atlantic coast for ever-grander wagers. All of this was described in covetous detail by the newspapers. The expenses and tragedies of the Civil War interrupted

these excesses for a few years, but things were back to normal in the season of 1866 with a long series of wild, tight, high-stakes match races. The last of these was sailed in a gale on October 9 from New York to Cape May, New Jersey, and return between two 108-footers, James Gordon Bennett, Jr.'s six-year-old *Henrietta* and Pierre Lorillard's new centerboarder *Vesta*. Both boats suffered damage, *Vesta's* so heavy that she was forced to heave-to for repairs for an hour, which was *Henrietta's* winning margin. However exciting, though inconclusive, those matches were, the 1866 New York racing season was upstaged by *Alice*, a little 53′ Massachusetts-based sloop. *Alice* made a well-publicized 19-day cruise across the Atlantic under the command of Captain Arthur H. Clark (who would later write a distinguished history of yachting) with a crew that included Charles A. Longfellow, the son of the poet Henry Wadsworth Longfellow.

NAUTICAL QUARTERLY

A colored engraving issued by William Foster on January 25, 1867, only a month after *Henrietta*'s arrival in England, shows the gallant schooner yacht sailing with aplomb in big seas.

So when a few of New York's young sporting bloods got together over a bottle in the Union Club on October 26 they had much to talk about. Before long, Pierre Lorillard and Franklin Osgood, owner of the fast new 106′ keel schooner *Fleetwing*, were engaged in one of those half-bragging, half-joking disputes about the relative merits of their vessels that, like most arguments about the boats of the day, focused on the seaworthiness of centerboards. Osgood allowed that Lorillard's wide, shallow *Vesta* might be fast in sheltered water, but could she, he baited, beat the deep, narrow *Fleetwing* in the open sea? Could *Vesta*, in fact, *survive* the open sea?

The conversation inevitably wound around to the "put-up or shut-up" stage. No doubt challenged by *Alice*'s feat, Lorillard and Osgood found an excuse to sail across the Atlantic: Emperor Napoleon III of France had scheduled a regatta to coincide with the 1867 Paris world's fair. When the evening finally staggered to its end, each side had agreed on a transatlantic match race to start at New York and finish at the Needles, the stalky chalk rocks on the west tip of the Isle of Wight. The stakes had risen to $30,000 a side, much more than the cost of one of the yachts. They would start seven weeks later on December 11—December, after all, being a good month for wind.

A day or two later, young Jamie Bennett heard about the race, the

THE HENRIETTA, VESTA AND FLEETWING ON THEIR WAY TO EUROPE
STAKE NINETY THOUSAND DOLLARS

extravagances of which were right up his alley. His request to join in, to bring the stakes to $90,000, was accepted. The proposed event fascinated all who heard of it because the figure was so high and because the intentions of the men involved were ambiguous. That they could cover their losses was taken for granted. Lorillard dominated the tobacco business; Osgood's father-in-law was the railroad and shipping baron "Commodore" Cornelius Vanderbilt; and Bennett's father owned the successful New York Herald. But what the public seemed more interested in was whether these tycoons would risk their necks in addition to their cash on the North Atlantic in winter. Bennett announced that he definitely would sail on board *Henrietta*. But as autumn chilled to winter the two originators of the project decided, not unreasonably, that racing across the North Atlantic in late December was not good for one's health. Lorillard's withdrawal attracted widespread criticism that he was interested only in free advertising for his snuff; one paper only half-jokingly worried that "the *Vesta* will perhaps carry sails emblazoned with the words *Lorillard Tobacco*." With the memory still fresh that *America* had been unloaded at a profit after only two races, some detractors opined that it would be ungentlemanly if, as was rumored, the owners planned to sell their yachts in Cowes (the excuse of the French regatta having quickly faded from memory).

In sum, the whole escapade seemed too outsized and commercial for a gentleman's sport. Commodore William H. McVickar initially refused to have the name of the New York Yacht Club sullied with what promised to be a crude combination of outlandish stakes and big profits. However, at a special meeting of the club called to discuss the matter, a member named Leonard Jerome gave a long, funny, pointed speech that brought McVickar and the doubters around. To quote from the minutes, which were given a full column in the Herald, "the question involving the right of gentlemen to bet on the race or to dispose of their boats was mooted."

Of all the extravagant characters involved with this extravagant event, Leonard Jerome is, in many ways, the most appealing. A 49-year-old stock market speculator who had made and lost a couple of fortunes, he was a part-owner of the New York Times and a former American consul to Trieste, Italy. He was also a well-known man-about-town and sportsman who had recently co-founded the American Jockey Club and built a race track, Jerome Park, in the Bronx. Besides winning the yacht club's endorsement for the race, Jerome succeeded in convincing the doubting Commodore McVickar to serve as the race's official judge. The competitors showed their gratitude and trust in Jerome by naming him the stakes holder, and he, in turn, convincingly demonstrated his faith in their risky enterprise by sailing as a guest of Bennett's on *Henrietta*. It is just possible that Jerome's interest may have been tickled by the fact that he controlled the Atlantic Telegraph Company, whose newly laid transatlantic cable promised to receive excellent publicity by winging the race results to New York.

To command their vessels, the owners hired the best captains they could find. Dick Brown, *America*'s skipper when she won the Hundred Guinea Cup, signed aboard *Fleetwing*. He resigned, however, three days before the start to protest being listed below Albert Thomas, the navigator, on the vessel's clearance papers. The result of his resignation was that Thomas took over the command in fact as well as name. The skipper of *Vesta* was George Dayton, an experienced, cautious squarerigger captain and father of 17. To keep an eye on him, Lorillard sent along his 20-year-old brother, George. The real coup, however, was Bennett's. For a fee of $7500 he brought on the great Samuel Samuels, holder of the transatlantic record under sail on the clipper *Dreadnought*. Dapper and calm on first acquaintance, Samuels had in 30 years at sea honestly earned the nickname "Bully," and was guaranteed to drive his men, his yacht, and himself to their limit.

Each skipper signed up a crew of 22—no easy task because of the combination of December and competition, either one of which alone might have been tolerable to a professional seaman, but both of which together made even strong men think of warm fires and a family Christmas. Samuels may have lived up to his nickname too soon, for *Henrietta*'s crew walked off the job a few days before the start of the race. According to one newspaper, "their places had to be supplied by a lot of landlubbers, few of whom could climb a mast."

On all three yachts the long tillers were replaced with more manageable worm-gear steering wheels. On *Henrietta* and *Vesta*, Samuels and Dayton strengthened the hulls and slightly cut down the towering rigs and, anticipating heavy seas, built strong shelters over the cockpits. *Fleetwing*, however, received little special attention due, perhaps, to the confusion over her command.

Along with the professional seamen sailed the owner or his representative, a few guests, and an observer from each of the other competitors—cheating not being unheard of then as well as now. Besides Jerome and Charles Longfellow (making his second transatlantic passage of the year), *Henrietta* took along Stephen Fisk, a reporter from the Herald, who was smuggled aboard at the last moment to avoid being served a subpoena to appear at a trial in Manhattan. Fisk's crusty boss, old James Gordon Bennett, had assigned him the dubious beat with these less-than-encouraging words: "This race. Yachts. One of 'em me son's. Cover it. Fall in the sea for all I care but get the news. Properly. Understood?" Since wild 26-year-old Jamie Bennett was little help around the office, perhaps the old man hoped that both men would fall in the sea together. It would make good headlines.

What with the weeks of anticipation and an estimated $1 million in bets circulating among the bookies, the start was crowded with spectator boats. It was rumored that one vessel was carrying an English detective searching

THE HENRIETTA THE WINNER

The Voyage Made in Thirteen Days and Twenty-Two Hours Mean Time

HER ARRIVAL AT COWES ON CHRISTMAS DAY

out an exiled Irish revolutionary named James Stephens, who he thought was about to be smuggled home in one of the yachts. Even if this were true, nothing could have been done about it in all the confusion. The three boats slipped their tows, set sail, and finally started to a hail of cannon fire and cheers at 1 p.m., December 11, 1866, rapidly broad-reaching away on the strong westerly that would hold for almost the entire race. The westerly gradually built to a grim, cold, snowy gale that shook the boats so badly that Leonard Jerome was heaved out of his bunk onto the hot cabin stove. Fortunately, in doing so, he knocked over a bucket of water which, along with his blanket, protected him from burns. Not at all fazed by this near-miss or by his surroundings ("mournful and depressing," according to Fisk), Jerome sipped champagne with one hand and held on tight with the other, while he informed Fisk about his relations with his mistress and his wife. Although Stephen Fisk was a hard-bitten police and war correspondent (it was he who recorded the last words of Stonewall Jackson, at Chancellorsville, "Let us cross over the river and rest under the shade of the trees"), he was taken aback by Jerome's frankness. Of Jerome's company, Fisk later wrote in his autobiography, "These seemed curiously intimate revelations to make in the cabin of a tiny yacht tossed about by a brewing gale in the middle of the Atlantic."

After a week of hard but controlled days of sailing 220 miles per day and more, the yachts were scalded when the southwest gale boiled over on December 18. Wave after wave swept *Henrietta*, the narrow leader, running at 9 knots under forestaysail and double-reefed foresail. She took so much water below through her deadlights that Samuels had the ship's carpenter drill holes in the cabin sole to drain the wash into the bilge. At 8:40 p.m. a huge breaker dropped on her, stove in a boat, and squeezed so much ocean through her deck seams and ports that the already nervous carpenter went berserk and screamed that the yacht was breaking up. The icily calm Bennett and Samuels kept panic from spreading among their inexperienced crew, but secretly worried that "the little plaything" (as Samuels called the 200-ton schooner) might break up. They had the storm trysails brought up from the cabin and bent on, and hove her to. For 13 hours she lay "lazily and pleasantly," according to Fisk, until the sea was all but calm. Anything but a bully as he nursed his ship through the storm, Samuels then turned east and recommenced living up to his reputation. By 9 a.m. on the 19th *Henrietta* was scudding off under her huge squaresail.

Fleetwing tragically bore the brunt of the storm. At about 9 p.m. on the 18th, just after the change of watch, a wave knocked her over until her upper shrouds lay in the sea and water covered her main companionway. The two helmsmen and six men huddling in the exposed cockpit were knocked overboard so violently that the helmsmen took some wheel spokes with them. Two men saved themselves by grabbing some rigging, but the other six were lost. Down below, the sailing master and mate crawled forward to and up through a small companionway. They made their way aft on deck, where they were greeted by the grim sight of the empty cockpit and the mangled steering wheel. The survivors hove-to for five hours and searched fruitlessly for their lost shipmates. Then they set as much sail as the dying storm would allow them to carry and resumed racing on a track to the south of their competitors.

Vesta endured the gale by scudding northeast before it, possibly because Captain Dayton felt that the centerboarder lacked sufficient stability to heave-to safely. During the night she crossed *Henrietta*'s wake and soon passed her—a success that, had it been known, might have eased tensions in *Vesta*'s afterguard. George Lorillard had been loudly critical of Dayton's seamanship almost since the start; when not berating him for having too much sail set in the gale, he was hounding him to shake out reefs. On the 20th Lorillard ordered the gray-bearded seaman to his cabin, where, as the 20-year-old recorded in his journal, "I told him that it was desirous that he should take my advice occasionally about making sail and make his officers hurry the men, as it was much to his benefit." Dayton's passionate response to this no doubt patronizingly offered advice was that, as far as he was concerned, the schooner could go to hell after reaching Cowes. Perhaps Lorillard would have been less critical of Dayton had he known that on the 20th *Vesta* lengthened her slim lead by making 277 miles while her competitors each logged only 260.

Vesta's real problem lay not with how hard or gently she was driven, but with her captain's strategy. She alone had run off before the gale, and was by far the most northerly of the three schooners, about 30 miles above the latitude of the Bishop Rock, the turning mark toward the Channel that lies in the Isles of Scilly. This seemed a safe enough course in the prevailing westerlies, so Dayton simply aimed at the rock and let *Vesta* fly. But on *Henrietta*, which came out of the storm about 20 miles south of *Vesta* and 10 above the Bishop's latitude, savvy Bully Samuels had different plans. A human pilot chart who knew this route blindfolded, Samuels predicted that the wind would back into the southeast as he neared Europe. Anticipating the wind shift, he trimmed sheets and steered several degrees high of the rhumb-line course, sacrificing a little speed in order to make the southing that, when the wind backed, would later allow him to reach around the Scillies rather than beat up to them. Some 100 miles astern and even farther to the south, Captain Thomas of *Fleetwing* duplicated Samuels' strategy.

On a warm, spring-like December 24 the wind did indeed back. *Vesta* had to come on the wind and beat with painful slowness into the first head sea of the trip. Realizing that she could not fetch the Bishop, Dayton came about to port tack, sailed off at almost a right angle to the rhumb line, then tacked back to slog into it some more. At 6:55 on Christmas Eve her crew finally saw the Bishop light barely off her lee bow, and Dayton, worried about running aground, continued to squeeze the wind with flat sails. All this reduced George Lorillard to imprecations that would have been even

THE FLEETWING AND VESTA ARRIVE DECEMBER 26
A Grand and Enthusiastic Reception
SIX MEN DROWNED FROM THE FLEETWING

more venomous had he known that, although Jamie Bennett had made his landfall at 7:45, thanks to Samuels' careful planning, he was now flying toward the rock on a 13-knot reach. *Henrietta* rushed by the pinching, pitching centerboarder in the dark and at 10:00 turned the Bishop and roared toward the Isle of Wight. *Vesta* finally inched around at midnight, having lost three hours to her competitor in only five hours of sailing. With *Fleetwing* last around at 4:40 Christmas morning, the three boats were separated by less than seven hours after almost 3,000 miles.

None of this was known to the competitors, who had not seen each other since soon after the start. Only when a pilot scrambled aboard *Henrietta*, gawking at the cloud of sail she was carrying in the small gale, did Bennett and Samuels learn they were first. At 3:46 on Christmas Day *Henrietta* swept by the Needles, having covered 3,106 miles in 13 days, 21 hours, 55 minutes. So good was Samuels' navigation that the total distance covered was only 40 miles more than the great circle distance. Her best day's run was a whopping 280 miles, while her average day's run of 223 miles gave her an average speed of 9.3 knots. Leonard Jerome promptly returned Jamie Bennett's wager and presented him with a bank draft for $60,000.

And *Vesta*? As Captain Dayton had hoped, she did go to hell, or at least to the racing sailor's version of those infernal regions. After losing some time taking a pilot aboard in the rough seas, Lorillard learned that *Henrietta* had already come by. This news, he wrote in his journal, "completely crushed us, and with drooping heads and broken hearts we quietly slunk away into our cabin to hold sad converse over our blighted hopes." As if that weren't enough, the pilot—whom Lorillard was convinced was either a drunk or a drug addict—directed Dayton around the wrong side of the Isle of Wight. The result was that Vesta lost a sufficient amount of time in frustrating backtracking to finish 12 hours behind *Henrietta* and three behind the fast-finishing *Fleetwing*.

While the crews celebrated Christmas with varying degrees of promptness and joy in Cowes Roads, problems with the transatlantic cable kept New York from hearing the results until the 30th. Ever since the start, the betting line had swooped and dived depending on whose rumors were believed when. Even old James Gordon Bennett was dragged into the hoopla. He had the Herald run off ten thousand flyers celebrating his son's daring, and spent his evenings with Pierre Lorillard and George Osgood conjecturally sailing backgammon pieces across charts of the North Atlantic and guessing how New York's weather would affect the yachts two or three days later. When the news finally reached America, the response was almost identical to the jingoism that had greeted the triumph of *America* in 1851. Cries of "young America triumphant" rang through sermons, editorial pages, and letters to the editor for weeks. Every actual and rumored detail of the race was covered with infinite care; even the yachts' logs were published. The British newspapers, as in 1851, were taken aback by the Americans' daring. They promptly dealt with its implied smudge on the national character with a mixture of self-criticism ("Our yachtsmen take things comfortably...") and damning-with-faint-praise ("We would not for a moment entertain a thought of depreciating this extraordinary Atlantic match and voyage, but...").

There was a grand dinner at Cowes' Gloucester Hotel where Jamie Bennett and Samuel Samuels offered gratifyingly humble speeches. Leonard Jerome delivered himself of another witty, rambling monologue meandering toward the satisfying conclusion that the world's salvation depended upon Anglo-American unity. (A few years later, Jerome acted on this ideal by marrying his pretty daughter, Jennie, off to the Duke of Marlborough, and soon becoming the grandfather of their son, Winston Leonard Spencer-Churchill.) Before leaving Cowes, Jerome made two financial contributions; he joined the owners and other guests in a subscription for the families of the six dead sailors, and presented Samuels with the deed for a house. That the house was worth $25,000 and the fund eventually totaled all of $5,800 suggests how priorities were ordered in those days.

Royalty played two small but significant parts in the celebration. Queen Victoria asked the Americans to sail in the Solent off Osborne House, her vacation home near Cowes, so she could see the victors in action. The English monarch formally received Commodore McVickar, expressing her sadness about the tragedy. This royal reception and other unforseen perqs impressed McVickar so much that he sent a note to the London Times bragging that he and he alone of all the Americans in Cowes had been so honored by the Queen. The sole controversy in the wake of the race surrounded Bennett's impetuous offer of *Henrietta* to Victoria's second son, Prince Alfred, the new Duke of Edinburgh. The gift was politely refused, and the American newspapers (other than the Herald) lambasted Bennett for not knowing his place. This adverse publicity did not stop the New York Yacht Club from electing him as Vice Commodore at the age of 26. The event's most lasting contribution was to Anglo-American goodwill, which had disappeared during the Civil War, when the British favored the Confederacy. The three schooners sailed home but were soon followed to England by another, *Sappho*, whose two summers of racing on the Solent stimulated Thomas Ashbury to make the first challenge for what was then called the Queen's Cup. In 1870 Ashbury's *Cambria* narrowly beat the Bennett-owned, Samuels-commanded *Dauntless* in a race to New York but then was overwhelmed by a wave of American schooners in the race for the Cup. Of the three yachts that sailed in the amazing great ocean race of 1866, only the tragic *Fleetwing* competed in the first America's Cup contest, finishing right behind the challenger in ninth place. While the place this single race holds in yachting history has been overshadowed by the subsequent America's Cup contests, this first transatlantic race was a bold, extravagant venture entirely in keeping with the wild energy of 'sixties yachting in New York.

NORMA JAY: WEST COAST IMPRESSIONS

BY REBECCA SMITH

Asked to think of images of nautical activity, few would see in their mind's eye a quiet harbor scene, fishboats in their slips, sailboats at a marina pier. Images of a race, or a cruising yacht thrashing through a storm, or even a capsize, would more likely jump to mind, for we tend to associate activity with motion or speed.

But there is activity to what seems inactive on the water. It is the activity of light. As every yachtsman or beachcomber has observed, the world on or near the water is an explosion of light from a myriad of reflecting surfaces—the water, a boat's white topsides, a dock's pilings, foul-weather gear. This nautical world of light is the world of "passive activity" that California artist Norma Jay captures in her impressionistic marine oil paintings of the fishing villages and marinas along the West Coast.

When Jay paints fishboats, workboats or sailboats, they are most often in repose—at anchor, tied to a wharf, or moving so slowly they seem to be becalmed. But if the subjects of her art are physically at rest, the paintings themselves are alive with the pulsating patterns of light and its colorful reflections—of hull mirrored on water, not as a dark shadow, but lambent with color, of water shimmering in the hues of the rainbow.

It is Jay's use of color that helps give her paintings their distinctive Western look. Jay juxtaposes short bursts of unmixed color on her large canvases, and from a distance the colors blend and fuse to create new hues. This is a technique borrowed from Impressionism, the style of painting Jay's work most nearly resembles, although, to be more precise, the artist describes what she does as "impressionistic realism." "It's sort of using the impressionistic style of painting, but it's a little more realistic," she explains.

The Impressionists, while much maligned in their 19th-century milieu, revolutionized painting with their assertion, among others, that color was modified by the light it was in. Jay's characteristic bold use of color reflects the unique quality of light on the West Coast, and helps associate her work in feeling with its locale. "There is an entirely different atmosphere along the West Coast than there is in the East. The Pacific Ocean is undoubtedly bluer than the Atlantic and it requires a lot more color," she says.

While Impressionism is a style of painting eminently suited for what Jay does—depicting the sensuous, richly lit world of the waterfront—this is not entirely the reason the California artist uses it. There is an idiosyncratic impetus for her to paint impressionistically. "I'm allergic to turpentine. It makes my fingers break out," the oil painter confesses, with a bravado akin to the swimmer who admits he's allergic to water. Using a palette knife, she applies the oils straight from the tube, and avoids turpentine entirely. "There are a lot of people who paint with a palette knife, but not really in my style."

Although Jay has been a professional marine painter for the past 15 years, she wasn't always one, nor was she always an artist. Inspired by her mother who was a "very fine pianist," Jay's first aspirations were to be a singer. "From the time I was very small I always was drawing, but I thought I was headed for a musical career because I had quite a lot of recognition in college. But," the artist recalls, "my grandfather used to say, 'No, no, you should become an artist, you should major in art.'"

Instead, Jay minored in art while at Wichita State University in her native Kansas. There, and later at the Art Institute of Chicago and at California State University in Long Beach, she learned the basics of drawing. This formal training, with a concentration on nude drawing, is evident in her marine work. Even though she doesn't often include people in her marine paintings, one of Jay's strengths, and something that sets her work apart from that of many contemporary marine artists, is her fine rendering of the human figure.

Shortly after she was married, Jay abandoned her dream of a life on stage because of the demands that such a career would make on her home life. "I come from a broken home, and I just wasn't going to have that in my own family," she explains, then adds, "I can't stand to do anything unless I do it well." She took her considerable creative energies and focused them on painting, something she could do without jeopardizing her home life. "At the time, though, I was not any particular type of artist."

What led subsequently to Norma Jay's full-time career in marine painting was her introduction to boats and the water while she and her husband, Laurence, an engineer, and their two daughters, were living in Sandusky, Ohio. There the Jays belonged to a yacht club and were part owners of *Indian Drum*, a 28' sloop. "My husband was sailing a Thistle-class sailboat on Lake Erie. He and a friend were entering all the races," she remembers. Always eager to share her husband's interests, Jay found herself drawn to the water. "I just found that I was spending more and more time around the water. I found it exciting."

A few years after Jay moved to California, where her husband was transferred to Ford Aerospace in Newport Beach, she began to put Western coastal and harbor scenes on canvas. Not long after she started painting marine subjects professionally, Jay began to receive recognition for her work. She is now invited frequently to exhibit in galleries and shows on both coasts. She is included in *The Dictionary of Sea Painters*, compiled by the curator of the National Maritime Museum in London, and is listed in *Who's Who In American Art*, which brings up

True to the influences of Impressionism, marine artist Norma Jay's paintings emphasize light and time of day. In the painting shown on pages 28 & 29, Jay records a portion of the waterfront at Morro Bay, which lies about 150 miles north of Los Angeles. It is late afternoon—the traditional time for cocktails—hence the title "Happy Hour." "Sunlight washing rows of neat white boats. Sunlight with bright blue skies casting abstract patterns and shimmering reflections over the rippling water." These are Jay's impressions of yachts and small fishboats in a Santa Barbara marina, the setting for "Light Impressions," above.

an interesting point about Jay's work within the context of its genre.

The appeal of her paintings is not, as is most marine art, limited to yachting enthusiasts and art collectors. Its appeal is wider. "People from all walks of life purchase Norma's work simply because they like it," says Sam Ehrenberg, partner in Atelier Galerie, a gallery in Carmel, California, that handles her paintings.

Whenever the artist goes exploring harbors and stretches of coast in California, Washington, and Oregon, she takes along sketch pad and camera. These tools of the trade record scenes which will give her ideas for what to paint, a decision which for Jay is a capricious one. "It's just a matter of what I'm in the mood to do at the time," she says, but concedes she does have a preference. "There's something about the atmosphere around little fishing harbors that I find intriguing," the artist says of the subjects she finds herself most often painting.

The locale of "Rising Tide," opposite, is Astoria, Oregon, a fishing port at the mouth of the Columbia River. The harbor is large and supports a sizeable fleet of commercial fishing vessels. "Evening on the Bay," above, reveals the artist's skills in depicting the human figure. The spot is the tranquil village of Morro Bay. "The sizeable, natural harbor has a small entrance," Jay explains, "and is protected by sand dunes. Fishing boats and pleasure craft provide the bulk of the marine activity as the harbor is not deep enough for ocean freighters."

The red powered dories in "Painted Ladies," Jay's oil above, are shrimp boats at Newport, Oregon, where all such craft are painted this vibrant color. This painting hangs in the lobby of an accounting firm amidst red leather chairs and crimson carpeting. "Harbor Sunshine," at right, is another scene from the Morro Bay waterfront, a favorite subject of Norma Jay's art. In a break from her West Coast impressions, Jay has been painting shrimp boats on the Gulf Coast, too. In addition to her painting, Jay has joined four other artists in operating a gallery where she sells her paintings and lithograph prints. The address is: The Back Door Gallery, 1406 South Coast Highway in the Art Center, Laguna Beach, CA 92651.

Before she applies her oils, Jay sketches her composition on the canvas, first in charcoal, then in acrylic. It will take her one to two weeks from her initial sketch before the painting is ready to be hung on the wall. The size of her paintings averages 30″ x 40″, ideal for her, she says, "because it gives me a little more freedom."

Norma Jay will rarely do more than 20 paintings a year, which leaves her the time to devote to one of her hobbies. "My husband and I are lapidary fans," she says. There is a pause. "We're rockhounds," she explains. Her husband cuts, grinds and polishes the stones, many of which they find themselves, and she makes jewelry out of them.

Even though Jay seems more content with her life then the average person, she too, asks herself "what next?" And she has an answer to her question. "I want to go to the Orient. I want to paint the old junks," she replies. While this trip may be several years in the offing, next year she and her husband plan to visit the Northeast and Nova Scotia. There she will do what she does so vividly for the West Coast—capture on canvas the sensuous, richly lit world of the waterfront.

A powerboat at 50 or 60 years is in its ripe old age. Classic cruisers and runabouts from the 'twenties and 'thirties are survivors, witnesses to careful management, loving care. With so much attention paid to these glamorous old boats now, it is strange to realize that, if 50 or 60 years is an unusual and desirable age for motorboats, it is an even more remarkable condition of longevity for motorboat builders. □ Only two builders of powerboats who advertised in Motor Boating magazine in 1930 are still building today: Chris-Craft and Huckins. Chris-Craft, one of the earliest names in motorboat building, has changed ownership several times, stayed alive with generous corporate backing during the 1960s and 1970s, and recently entered a new stage of product expansion with the help of innovative management and broad funding. The Huckins Yacht Corporation, on the other hand, has stayed in the family. Through the years, Huckins has built a distinctive style of motor yacht that has remained remarkably constant, hardly straying from the concept of a fast, lightweight, seagoing hull envisioned by its founder, Frank Pembroke Huckins, in the late 1920s. It may be that the character and philosophy behind this family firm are the ingredients that have kept it alive and well when so many other yards have passed away. And Huckins has been fortunate in two other, perhaps corollary, ways: there has been constant effective leadership, and the company has had the capability of making timely, significant changes in the technology of their work.

A lightweight, vee-bottom runabout hull made large was the essence of the Huckins design philosophy, and it was brought off with innovative laminated-wood technology in shaping frame members and hull skin for a boat that was light, fast, slightly flexible, and remarkably durable. More than 300 of the 430+ Huckins yachts built since 1928 are believed to be still in commission. The man who started it all is shown at right with a trademark pipe in his teeth—Frank Pembroke Huckins. With him aboard a Huckins PT is Henry Skinner Baldwin, vice president of the yard.

NAUTICAL QUARTERLY

HUCKINS

ALIVE AND WELL AT 56

BY STANLEY ROSENFELD

Old and new activity at the Huckins yard in Jacksonville: Below, craftsmen apply double-diagonal runs of mahogany over an oak skeleton whose frames were sawn and keel/stem laminated. All of the Huckins wood hulls were built with this diagonally-laid double skin of mahogany, following PT-boat specs, after World War II. Planks were glued with Borden's phenolic resin and clench nailed, as shown here, then screw-fastened to frames, chines, clamps and keel. Hull thickness was 3/4" to 1¼", and in 1961 a finishing touch in the form of fiberglass cloth laid in epoxy resin was adopted. The photos above show Huckins in the fiberglass era. Above left, a new 58′ Kirkline sportfisherman receives finishing touches, and above center a hull mold made from laths is moved into a shed where Airex foam and fiberglass cloth will be applied to pop out a fiberglass-sandwich hull. The hull design, as can be seen, is in the Huckins tradition of modified-vee, with a virtually flat planing surface aft. Airex/fiberglass construction also carries on the Huckins tradition of light weight combined with durability. Above are the company's 1984 principals: from left to right, Ken Archibald, Cindy Purcell, Ed Cameron and Buddy Purcell.

In 1923, Frank Pembroke Huckins sold the P.S. Huckins Company, a family timber business founded in 1833. The old company was formed to furnish planking, wedges, hackmatack knees and locust treenails to the builders of sailing vessels that still carried much of the cargo moving along the Atlantic coast. Huckins's parents summered at the shore in Duxbury, Massachusetts, and were financially able and philosophically inclined to let their young son indulge his childhood interest in boatbuilding. It was a part of his life before he was in his teens, and his years at Harvard's School of Engineering provided him with a technical base to pursue his passion more seriously.

Frank Pembroke Huckins moved to Jacksonville in 1924, and in 1926 he invested in the Drayer-Warren Company, which then became the Warren-Huckins Company, an architectural millwork firm busy supplying the construction boom roaring in Florida in the mid-to-late 1920s. At the time, he began to think of the potential of the millwork shops for going into production-line boatbuilding. During the next two years, Huckins reorganized his personal and business life. He was divorced for the second time and married Betty Archibald, bought Warren's share of the Warren-Huckins Company, founded the Huckins Yacht Corporation in 1928, and designed and built the first Huckins for himself, a 42′ twin-screw motor yacht that cruised at 20 knots.

That summer, he cruised in his new yacht from Jacksonville to New England, a cruising pattern he would follow throughout his life. On this cruise he contemplated the state of his affairs and made some plans for the future. He wrote a letter shortly after arriving in New York to a friend who had been the navigator aboard, and it reveals the state of his mind and the rationale that brought him to boatbuilding. The letter discussed the financial problems arising from the settlement of his divorce while at the same time buying out his partner in business. "My real trouble is economic worry," he wrote. "I am in serious danger of licking myself... due to my frozen assets, and I fight that all the time, and the fighting wears me... I am satisfied that I cannot command the amount of necessary capital we both agreed was essential to doing the yacht business RIGHT. I am therefore facing the alternative of a) Cutting my cloth according to the goods; building boats only on order; playing a long, cautious waiting game, or b) Abandoning an highly speculative future in yacht building and trying to find a less ambitious niche, not as a principal, in some existing business.

"The objection to b) is that it probably means leaving Jacksonville and going back North where my services would command a higher price, and I had almost rather remain in Jacksonville and starve than leave it." Huckins chose to remain in Jacksonville and build boats, although he didn't build boats exactly to order.

His concept of the ideal cruising powerboat was a planing hull that would cruise at about 20 knots. To Huckins, the displacement hull with its strict limitations on speed made no sense at all. A planing cruiser differs significantly from a displacement type. At a critical speed—about 10 knots in the case of a 45-footer with adequate power, light weight and proper bottom design—the planing hull will rise up and displace less than its own weight. It will skim on the surface, riding partially on the water rather than in it. With the same power, it will go faster than a displacement hull and be reasonably stingy with fuel. Huckins hulls have always been comparatively light, with a sharp bow section forward that fairs through strong planing sections to a rather flat section at the transom. The problem in maintaining excellent performance in cruising-sized planing boats has been keeping them light in weight.

In 1929, using a small booth at the Motor Boat Show in New York and some clever advertising copy, Huckins secured orders for six twin-screw 45-footers, a tremendous financial boost to his infant yard. These initial sales provided so strong a sense of believability to his future as a boatbuilder and salesman that it carried him through the worst years of the Depression. Another early-'thirties gambit was a 25′ bargain-priced Huckins that sold well in hard times. By 1935, the economy as it affected the boating world had so improved that Huckins doubled production over 1934. From then until the war years, the yard was building more than ten boats a year. In the boom year of 1937, the Huckins Yacht Corporation built 21 of their distinctive Fairform Flyers—spare, clean-lined cruisers that were described as "symbols of yacht perfection" in the company's advertising.

From hull number one, Huckins cruisers have always had a keel and stem laminated in a single form. The frames were Appalachian sawn oak, with a few exceptions that made use of steam-bent or laminated frames. The prewar hulls were batten-seam construction, with topsides of single-planked mahogany, bottoms double-planked with a glued canvas lining between runs of relatively thin wood. All of the early hulls were powered with Kermath engines. The construction of the hulls, although light in weight, proved with time to be strong, and their bottom design made good their designer and builder's claims to deliver both speed and fuel economy with moderate power. With his intuitive understanding of the value of a trade name, Frank Pembroke Huckins called his hull form "the Quadraconic Hull."

In the boom year of 1937, the Huckins Yacht Corporation built 21 of their distinctive Fairform Flyers—spare, clean-lined cruisers that were described as "symbols of yacht perfection."

He never explained what "Quadraconic Hull" meant, other than that it was the proper name of special formulae for "...four conical intersections that generate a specific form of hull." The phrase was used in all his advertising and literature, and it seems to have been impressive to his clients. His competitors considered it nothing more than advertising copy. Although Huckins was on occasion irascible and irritating, he never failed to be interesting; he was a colorful character who gathered a loyal following of owners, many of whom became repeat customers. They knew that his boats performed as he said they would, and they were satisfied with their functional, although sometimes austere, interior arrangements and furnishings.

The often-boxy exterior profiles of Huckins yachts were characteristically similar, and were easily recognized all along the Atlantic coast from Florida to Maine. The boats were elite, but plain and functional, and they were admired even by those who called them "Squareform Flyers." Their owners were so loyal and partisan they could very well be considered members of a mystical and exclusive Huckins Yacht Club. Testimony to the care these owners gave their boats, and to the durability of Huckins hull construction, is the fact that more than 300 of 430+ Huckins yachts built since 1928 are believed to be still in commission. This is a remarkable record.

Today, many Huckins owners want all the household amenities aboard—dishwashers, freezers, garbage compactors, washing machines, tubs with Jacuzzi systems, and a full complement of electronics. Frank Huckins would spin in his grave if he could know how some of his yachts are loaded down now. He would not have permitted it. In many instances he refused an owner's demand to install equipment or fittings that he felt were unnecessarily heavy. If clients insisted, he told them to find another builder. From the beginning, he would tell an owner how one of his cruisers should properly be outfitted, and the essence of it was lightness. Early on, a curtain was just as good as a door, and a lightweight rattan chair better than a built-in settee.

Huckins was also a natural advertising copywriter. He had a way with words and a firm belief in the validity of his convictions. He wrote the copy in the attractive brochures he issued for each Huckins model, and it was often wonderful stuff. Of the galley in the 38' Sedan, he wrote: "No orphan stuck off in a dark and fetid corner, nor one of those trick affairs where you press a button and the stove falls on your foot, *this* galley was designed for the important purpose of inspiring luscious meals." Pointing up the lack of noise and vibration in Fairform Flyers, he wrote: "There are few boats in which the swish of the water is the dominant note. There are *no* other boats in which a young damsel can ride ninety miles sitting directly *atop the engine enclosure*, then innocently ask at the end of the trip where the engines were located. This *actually happened* in a Sportsman 36."

By the time World War II came along, Huckins was confident that he could build a better motor torpedo boat. After a struggle to get financing, he went ahead on his own, the U.S. Navy providing only the engines on loan, with no promise of a contract. Huckins did get an order from the Navy, and built 18 PT boats for the government, a project that kept the yard busy all through the war, although the Huckins PTs were used for training rather than combat.

In a speech delivered before the Great Lakes Cruising Club on April 24, 1944, Huckins revealed some of his PT experiences with a flash of the dry humor for which he was famous. It began: "My Dear Commodore and fellow Aquamaniacs: I thus address you because after nearly 50 years of observation I am convinced that nearly anyone who owns a boat is only a little less crazy than the man who tries to build them. However, I think we can agree that cruising is a mild, jovial, and rather beneficial form of insanity."

In describing the problems he had met, he said, "My trouble on the PT design was that I had not the slightest idea about armament and could not pry any information out of anybody." After building the hull, he said, "I found out what a PT boat really had to carry. It was only about ten tons more than I had guessed. The torpedo tubes were twice as big as I thought and loaded through the opposite end than I had assumed, so nothing fitted on the boat. Everything was ducky until we got her into a seaway. She had the flexibility of front-row chorus girls. When the bow rose, the stern stayed right where it was. She wagged her tail like my dog Fairfa. The funny part of it was that the boat did not break up, nor did she pound. The all-laminated construction bent—too damn much—but it didn't break."

Huckins corrected the excess flexibility of his PT hulls by placing an oak bellyband around the hull, parallel to and rising about ten inches above the chine. The hulls were diagonally double planked, both bottom and sides, the bottom inside planking 9/16ths of an inch, and the outside 11/16ths. This method of building in double-diagonal planking, and with stiffening at the chine, became standard in the wooden yachts Huckins built after the war. The PT program was a wonderful opportunity for Huckins to research and develop his concept of the way an ocean-going, high-speed planing hull of 70' and more should be designed and built. It was 25 years before the yard again built a hull as big as the Huckins 78' PT, but they were ready when the opportunity came. Toward the end of the

---

Huckins built 18 PTs for the government, a project that kept the yard busy all through the war, although the Huckins PTs were used for training rather than combat.

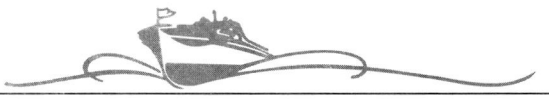

war, Huckins differed with the Navy about procedure and, in a form of protest, spent much of his time at the drawing board he kept at home, planning his program of postwar yacht design and building.

Right after the war, the plant was moved from downtown Jacksonville to a new site on the Ortega River. Yachtbuilding began immediately, with 10 new hulls in 1946 and 28 in 1947. The yard was humming as never before. In 1951, as Frank Pembroke Huckins was preparing for his annual cruise to the north, he died in his sleep of a cerebral hemorrhage. His sudden death evoked heartfelt responses from Huckins owners, many referring to "our beloved Huck." He was remembered as an individualist, a genius, an autocrat. He was described as a man of strong character, indomitable will, firmly held opinions, and yet with a rare sense of humor. The powers that be in powerboating agreed that he had a remarkable gift for designing seagoing boats. He was dominant in the life of the company, and though the sudden passing of such a forceful leader could have left the enterprise in chaos, this was not the case.

On Huckins's death, the vice president of the yard, Henry Skinner Baldwin, carried on. In a time of steady growth and stable technology, Baldwin steered a steady course. Ray Teller, chief engineer under Huckins, was expert in press and customer relations as well as engineering. He had some of the sense of showmanship so familiar in Huckins, and he proved a perfect foil to the more sober Henry Baldwin. During the first ten years of their stewardship, construction and sales continued at their usual pace. Huckins held its share of the market and customers were not wooed away by anything new in yachtbuilding style or technology.

However, fiberglass hulls introduced a new vocabulary and new possibilities to yacht owners, even though the new plastic technology was not initially welcomed in the Huckins yard. Early fiberglass construction produced a heavier hull than wood, and although there were maintenance advantages to fiberglass, particularly in the south, the extra weight all but ruled it out for Huckins. The yard also worried about introducing techniques of fiberglass building to a staff schooled in wood. Huckins wanted to keep its craftsmen happy, and fiberglass building threatened the good relationship that existed. But progress—if fiberglass was progress— could not be denied in the competitive boatbuilding world. In 1961, Huckins bowed to the inevitable and put a fiberglass sheath on a 53-footer then building. This became standard practice. The fiberglass served primarily as insulation between the wood and the elements. It also reduced the number of metal contacts with water and decreased the possibilities of electrolytic corrosion. For the next decade, Huckins owners were well satisfied with wood hulls in a fiberglass skin.

During the 1960s, there was a marked increase in builders competing for the attention of the limited group of yachtsmen who bought big cruising motorboats. The number of boats Huckins built annually decreased, but the size of the boats they built increased proportionately. In 1971, Kenneth Warren Archibald, stepson of Frank Pembroke Huckins, succeeded Henry Baldwin as president, and about this time Robert M. Steward succeeded Ray Teller as chief engineer. Once again, there was a complementary interaction of personalities and talents at the yard. Archibald was as steady as Baldwin, and Steward was innovative in a time that required innovation. Between them, they successfully carried Huckins to new construction methods and finally to new materials.

By the mid-1970s, new owners who were willing to build 60' power yachts in wood were becoming rare. In 1976, none came to the Huckins yard. Fiberglass and aluminum were in vogue, with owners convinced that either one would involve lower maintenance costs and bring higher resale value than wood. If the yard was to continue building, it would need to abandon wood and turn to a new material. After a good deal of soul-searching and research into wood, fiberglass and aluminum, they chose Airex-core fiberglass construction. The choice, Ken Archibald says, was "...due to not being able to sell wooden boats anymore. It was a matter of change or go out of business." At this critical moment, a loyal customer agreed to have her yacht built of Airex-core fiberglass, a testimony of faith in Huckins and a godsend to the yard. In 1977, the yard launched its first Airex hull, the 76' motor yacht *Deep Stuff*. Huckins has built 13 big motor yachts of Airex fiberglass construction since.

Airex proved to be the right choice for Huckins for both practical and aesthetic reasons. It is a rigid PVC (polyvinylchloride) closed-cell foam used in sandwich core construction. It can be worked very much like wood, and in practice Huckins has been able to build a hull even lighter than what was possible in wood. The yard was unwilling to use traditional fiberglass boatbuilding methods because single-skin fiberglass (that is, the usual laminate of fiberglass without an inner core), turned out a heavier boat than their diagonal-strip wood construction. With Airex, it was possible to save approximately one third of the fiberglass layup and put a sandwich core in the middle between two skins of fiberglass. The core provides panel stiffness, which one would expect in a cold-molded or aluminum boat, but it also provides sound and thermal insulation.

Huckins has always prided itself on the distinctive, patrol-boat appearance of its hulls. Aesthetically, Airex works in a way that permits Huckins to maintain the lines and character of its traditions, yet benefit

---

Early fiberglass construction produced a heavier
hull than wood, and although there were maintenance advantages to fiberglass,
the extra weight all but ruled it out for Huckins.

NAUTICAL QUARTERLY
FAIRFORM FLYER
SYMBOL OF YACHT PERFECTION

Thus we present everything that heart could desire — *Beauty* and *Silence* to soothe the soul — Moderate *cost* to fit today's income — *Smooth-Speed* to thrill the sophisticated — *Sublime Comfort* to appease the fastidious.

Nine Fairform Flyers from the 'thirties, 'forties and 'fifties are shown above. And at left, just for decoration, are bathing beauties from 1936 who brightened the pages of a Huckins catalog. The boats show a similarity of hull form but a wide variety of purposes and styles of house structure. Huckins yachts were built to standard hull designs, and to some extent standard models, but they were custom boats otherwise, and no two Huckins yachts were ever exactly alike. What they had in common were swiftness, durability, fine but spare workmanship below decks, and a straightforward patrol-boat style. There were no other powerboats quite like them, and they were recognizable wherever they went.

from the practical advantages of the new material. Customers love it, and the men in the shop, led by Buddy Purcell, are happy to work with it. Purcell is another example of the right person being at Huckins at a critical time. Buddy married Cindy Archibald, Ken Archibald's daughter, and came to work in the plant in 1970. He has a degree in chemistry, but left his field and half his income for a job at Huckins as a painter. For the next seven years, he worked in the carpentry, mechanical, purchasing and accounting departments, and is now vice president. He is a tinkerer, a builder and a problem-solver at heart, and he takes pleasure in working with his hands. Building boats in Airex and fiberglass fascinated Buddy Purcell, and he wanted to be part of it. Today, he says, "I lay up the hull. I go out there and actually put on the fiberglass, not as a director, as a worker."

The first Airex hull took weeks to lay up. The men in the plant, who had worked in wood all their lives, thought fiberglass an alien, awful material. Buddy saw it as a challenge, and he learned to enjoy working with it. He soon put together and inspired a crew that now shares his enthusiasm for foam/fiberglass boatbuilding. In one day five men together can make one layup of cloth that covers both sides of a 58' hull from sheer to sheer. With each new hull, Buddy carries the technology a step further, and he claims that each hull is stronger and lighter. In the words of Tom Johannsen of Torin, Inc., which imports Airex from Switzerland, Buddy "...has achieved a high glass content and a high-quality layup to maximize the strengths and minimize the weight...If Huckins can build a hull which is almost the same weight as what can be done with the super stuff—the big ovens and the pre-pregs—that really is a very significant achievement." Just what this means in pounds is graphically shown in a comparison of the weights of two yachts named *Bright Hour* built for Calvin Houghland. In 1971, Mr. Houghland had a 65-footer built of wood with a fiberglass-covered hull. The hull weight off the mold was 19,430 pounds. In 1983, Mr. Houghland's new *Bright Hour*, a 74' Airex/fiberglass hull, had a hull weight of 15,000 pounds. The bigger hull was 4430 pounds lighter.

Huckins yachts are custom-built, tailored to the owner's needs and desires. Just how different these can be is apparent in two recent 74' sport cruisers—*Poco Mas*, built in 1982, and *Bright Hour*, built in 1983. *Bright Hour*'s owner enjoys cruising and fishing throughout the Bahamas and the Caribbean. He usually has along a group of seasoned shipmates who have been on these adventures with him for many years. He has been all around the Caribbean, and sometimes *Bright Hour* is far from her home port. She is powered by twin 670-hp diesel engines that give her a cruising speed of 21 knots. With 1800 gallons of fuel, her range is 470 nautical miles at this brisk speed, and much more, of course, when running slower.

Poco Mas has an identical 74' sport-cruiser hull, but the superstructure, interior fittings and the service expected of her are quite different. Her owners live in Texas, and with a demanding business schedule taking most of their time, they find only short periods to be aboard. They enjoy stopping at the Ocean Reef Club in Key Largo and want to be able to get from there to the Huckins yard in Jacksonville—where they leave *Poco Mas* between trips—between dawn and dusk. This is a long day's journey of about 400 miles. *Poco Mas* is powered with twin 1000-horsepower TCX diesels, which give her a top speed of 35 knots. *Bright Hour* is a serious cruising/fishing yacht, and although *Poco Mas* can play the same role, she also has the potential for being a sporty 74' commuter, even a ski boat.

The present administration of Huckins, as so often in the past, combines a blend of complementary talents. Kenneth Archibald is now chairman of the board. Edward J. Cameron, president, has a long background in yacht sales and brokerage, which are becoming important Huckins activities, that is both the resale of older Huckins yachts and the sale of other builders' boats. Buddy Purcell is vice president and supervisor of construction. Cindy Archibald Purcell, treasurer, grew up under the live oaks that line the St. John's River not far from the plant's present location. Ken Archibald, her father, built a 12' outboard-powered plywood boat for her tenth Christmas. From then on, as she says, "I lived on the river. I never came off the water after that." After college and marriage to Buddy Purcell, she joined him in Alaska, where he was detachment commander of the 400-bed hospital at Fort Wainwright in Fairbanks. They both have adventurous spirits. In Alaska, they helped friends build a log cabin on the Arctic Circle, mined for gold, and made a river trip down the Chena. While Buddy worked at the hospital, Cindy took a job as a roofing and fencing estimator. "I would crawl on top of the roofs taking measurements and doing estimates on them, and going places no female should, but I had a lot of fun," she remembers. Their joy in discovery and in physical challenge is still with them.

When Cindy and Buddy returned to Jacksonville, they acquired a plot of ground along the shore of the St. John's, in an area where a stand of giant live oaks rise in a majesty rarely seen. Dappled sunlight filters through the outstretched arms of the trees and through Spanish moss, giving form in the vaulted space beneath to one of nature's unforgettable cathedrals. A contractor poured the concrete foundation and built the walls and roof of their home, but they put in the interior themselves. The Purcells live on the shore of the St. John's with their two daughters, Benham and Field. Cindy still periodically goes on Outward Bound trips. Lunchtime at the

---

The first Airex hull took weeks to lay up.
The men in the plant, who had worked in wood all their lives, thought fiberglass
an alien, awful material. Buddy saw it as a challenge...

Huckins plant usually finds Cindy and Buddy both in jogging togs, off on a five-mile run to keep in shape. With their engaging and open ways, they are superb representatives of Huckins.

Cindy says of the plant's future that they would like to stay within 74' overall in new boatbuilding. In 1980, they built an 86-footer, (*Kenlane*, shown and discussed in NQ 14), so they can successfully build a bigger yacht. But the larger the boats, the more heavily owners seem to load them, and Cindy Purcell feels that the facilities and philosophies of the plant are better suited to boats no bigger than the 74-footers. Modern powerboats are often used for elaborate entertaining, and Huckins plans new and beamier designs for such uses. And this builder of lightweight performance cruisers intends to stay with Airex. Buddy Purcell and his team are experimenting with new materials and new methods of building superstructures in order to make them lighter, and there are other areas of R & D; but, as Cindy says, "We will not make changes unless we find it beneficial."

Some changes have come naturally with time. Service work now accounts for 40% of Huckins activity. In recent months, *Summertime*, a 70-footer built by Derecktor; *Never A Doubt*, a 48' Rybovich; *Burwatt*, a 60' Trumpy; and *Great Grief*, a 54' Striker, have had work done in the yard. In a return to the yard's origins, Buddy keeps the carpentry shop busy in slow periods doing architectural millwork for builders in the area. Between the service and the millwork, they manage to keep their valued staff together through the cyclical flow of the custom-boatbuilding game.

A project that certainly would have evoked comment from Frank Pembroke Huckins is now in progress. Sam Brown, a retired naval aviator, came to Huckins with the unusual request that they build a 50-footer powered by four OMC Sea Drives. Brown chose Huckins because he thought they were capable of being innovative and solving problems with something that had never been tried before. His Sea-Drive Huckins—powered by four of OMC's 2.5-liter V6 outboards—is a radical departure from Brown's earlier boats. His first was a 48' wood trawler yacht, converted from a Long Island fishing boat. It did nine knots at best and, as Brown observed, "the engine was a little tired." Brown built a second trawler-type boat, *Island Queen*, for a combination of yachting and commercial fishing. She is 48' overall, has a 16' beam and is very brawny. "She's fairly heavy," Brown says. "She weighs 29 tons, and when I fished in her I had a 6000-pound fish box in the cockpit. I built her as a commercial boat to fish for red snapper, and fished for about two years."

Sam Brown first thought of the Sea Drives as an effective source of power when he read about an experimental application Bertram tried with one of their 31-footers. He became convinced of the advantages of a big outboard installation in a relatively big boat. "There are no through-hull fittings, no shafts, no rudders, no struts, no stuffing box, no oil exchanger, no fresh water to check—all the problems you have with an inboard installation," he argues. "You save a great deal of weight, and you also save a great deal of money. When it's sitting still, you pull the engines out of the water, so you don't get your underwater hardware all crudded up with barnacles, which is a real problem in this area. If you bump into something, the engines can come up, and even if you did damage your propellers, you can pull the engine up and change them rather than have the boat hauled out. You don't need to have your shafts aligned. It was the innumerable advantages to this idea that got me interested... We'll see how it works."

It took Brown a year and a half to persuade Huckins to start on his new boat. As Huckins researched the project, Jon Hall, their designer, began thinking about a hull that would be appropriate for Sea Drives. Hall felt that the conventional Quadraconic Hull of Frank Pembroke Huckins was not the right choice. The diesel engines normally installed on a 50-footer weigh 7000 to 8000 pounds, while the four Sea Drives total only 1500 pounds. The traditional 50-footer weighs about 40,000 pounds, whereas the 50-footer with Sea Drives will weigh 27,000 pounds. To get some hull under water, Hall developed an underbody with a 12-degree deadrise at the transom and a step chine along the side eight inches deep aft.

As Hall investigated multi-engine power applications, the stumbling block seemed to be the difficulty getting a hull powered by four engines to steer satisfactorily. This problem seems finally to have been overcome with a hydraulic installation engineered by HyDrive, an Australian firm that specializes in marine steering. It will use a HyDrive radial piston pump, an eccentric pump with four pistons working off-center, three ball valves between engines and the OMC-supplied cylinders attached to the Sea Drives. The advantage to this installation is that, once the system has been bled, it becomes a closed-loop recirculating system. The only way it can lose oil is through a loose fitting, a broken line or cylinder. It should provide positive steering control with no slop or slack.

With the steering problem solved, Jon Hall feels that the new *Island Queen* should get up on plane easily, steer securely and reach a speed of 29 knots. "The project is unique," says Hall. "The owner likes to try something different. He is a retired Navy person." Indeed he is. Sam Brown has had some experience with vessels other than his two trawler yachts: as Admiral Sam Brown, he commanded the *USS Forrestal* in 1959-60.

· Modern powerboats are often used for elaborate entertaining, and Huckins plans new and beamier designs for such uses. And this builder of lightweight performance cruisers intends to stay with Airex.

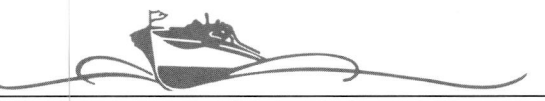

Frank Pembroke Huckins would tell his customers exactly how he was going to build their boats, and he didn't care if he made a sale. If they didn't agree with him, they could walk away. At Huckins today, the management isn't quite so autocratic. They understand that customers have needs, sometimes for a yacht that's unique, sometimes for a boat with a heavy load of extras aboard. Huckins is trying to hold to its traditional boatbuilding philosophy, and at the same time make it possible for a potential client to get the boat he wants. Huckins still advertises that the Quadraconic Hull can be driven with less power than other designs of similar size and give better fuel economy and performance. The management also thinks, as Frank Pembroke Huckins did, that they build a boat with graceful lines and good behavior. Cindy and Buddy Purcell are young, full of fun, hardworking, knowledgeable and very serious about the future of their company. The Fairform Flyer, an old and honored trade name in the powerboat market, will likely be around for a few decades more—maybe another five or six.

KRAFT V

A classic Huckins motor yacht, *Kraft V* was delivered in June of 1962 for Hugh Camp, chairman of the Union-Camp Corporation, a firm that makes everything from lunch bags to packaging materials from kraft paper. The new boat's name recognized the company's product, and she was a successor to *Kraft III*, an Offshore 48 delivered in 1947, and *Kraft IV*, a Linwood 53 built by Huckins in 1956.

A standard Huckins Offshore 64 with a foot of extra length at 65' overall, *Kraft V* was built to a bottom design that Frank Pembroke Huckins had laid down about 1945, a "Quadraconic" modified vee that remained unchanged for 30 years.

This hull weighed about 70,000 pounds at full load, certainly more than Frank Huckins would have approved, but most of her construction details were in keeping with the spare and simple traditions of the builder, as some of these photos show. Bulkheads and cabinets were ½" Duraply, with a surface coating made to take smooth coats of paint. Mahogany-faced ½" plywood was used for the helm console and for paneling in the deckhouse, and doubled runs of ½" plywood were used in the engine compartment. Soles were ½" plywood except in the deckhouse where ¾" was used. Deckhouse sides were also ¾" plywood. Decks were two layers of ⅜" plywood glued together. Fiberglass insulation was used throughout. A relatively heavy feature of this boat was the Masonite pegboard on most of her overheads, a sound-deadening material that Bob Steward regards as heavy, and also recalls was installed with "about two million small screws."

The hull was the slightly flexible and very durable double-diagonal lamination of mahogany adopted by Huckins after the war, with hull and decks finished off in fiberglass laid in epoxy resin. *Kraft V* was originally powered by twin G.M. 12V-71N diesels which developed 456 horsepower each in 1962. She carried 640 gallons of fuel and 200 gallons of water, and her top speed was just under 22 knots. She was later repowered with new 12V-71Ns of 500 hp.

Hugh Camp kept her at Hobe Sound, Florida, in the winter, and at Port Washington, Long Island, in the summer, and she saw considerable use in his ownership. She was sold to Arthur Heublein of the liquor importing firm in 1968 and renamed *Elixir*. As *Elixir*, she was a familiar sight on Long Island Sound, and in 1974 she was chartered by Joe Bartram and temporarily renamed *Excite*. She served as a support vessel to the *Courageous* syndicate in that America's Cup summer.

As these few 1962 photos show, *Kraft V/Elixir* was (and still is) an attractive and dead-functional coastal cruising machine in the Huckins tradition of efficient performance and crisp good looks. Below are an owner's stateroom and adjacent head and shower, aft under the deck lounge; a two-berth guest stateroom under the pilothouse, with its own head to port across the passage; a large deckhouse salon amidships with living-room furniture; a galley to port and dinette to starboard below the level of the deckhouse sole forward; then crew quarters for two with a head in the forepeak. The deck lounge is furnished like a porch with lightweight bamboo furniture, and a small wet bar is abaft the helm station with a bench seat built in forward. A low cockpit is aft over the engines.

Kraft V, still named *Elixir*, is alive and well at the age of 22, owned now by Dan Prior of Chagrin Falls, Ohio, and kept year 'round at Faro Blanco in the Florida Keys. The Priors spend about eight months of the year aboard, cruising frequently to places like the Dry Tortugas, the Florida Bay edges of the Everglades, and to the Bahamas. Her 1970 diesel engines were just rebuilt; she's had a new generator this year; and in June she spent some weeks in the Bahamas. "We use her quite a lot," says Mrs. Prior. "She's wonderful."

Representative of the Huckins motor yachts of the late 1950s and the 1960s, *Kraft V* is shown at her top speed of 20+ knots on page 45. On these pages are some of her spaces, photographed just after her launching in 1962. She's more elaborate than the yachts built by Frank Pembroke Huckins, and thus a bit heavier; in '62 her loaded weight was about 70,000 pounds, but this is still far lighter than fiberglass yachts in her size range being built today.

Shown here are two views of *Kraft V*'s owner's stateroom, at left and below, and the guest stateroom at right, good examples of Huckins workmanship and finish in Duraply.

LOA: 65'
Beam: 16'2"
Draft: 4'9"
Weight: 70,000 pounds, approx., at full load
Fuel: 640 gallons
Water: 200 gallons
Power: twin 456-hp G.M. diesels
Hull: laminated wood
Designer and builder: Huckins Yacht Corp., 3482 Lakeshore Blvd., Jacksonville, FL 32210

POCO MAS

Delivered in August of 1982, *Poco Mas* carries on the light, lean boatbuilding tradition represented by *Kraft V*. She's essentially a big, elegant speedboat, as the full-tilt photograph on the next two pages testifies, and Huckins engineers have timed her speed at just under 40 mph.

The all-up weight of this boat is 73,000 to 75,000 pounds in light trim, and about 82,000 pounds at half load. A conventional fiberglass motor yacht of similar dimensions would be 30,000 to 40,000 pounds heavier. *Poco Mas* is driven by two blue-printed G.M. 12V-71TI diesels prepared by TCX of Costa Mesa, California, sophisticated engines that deliver 1000 horsepower each through 1½:1 ZF vee drives.

Poco Mas is owned by Texas automobile dealers Bill Gardner and John R. Schuehle, who keep her at the Huckins yard in Jacksonville but like to explore the Florida Keys from bases at Ocean Reef and Marathon. "They just cruise and have fun with her," says Cindy Purcell. Gardner and Schuehle had previously owned two used Huckins yachts, and when they commissioned this one they asked for a boat with enough speed to zip from Key Largo to Jacksonville in an easy day and with a profile low enough to clear the bridge to go outside at Marathon.

As these few photos show, *Poco Mas* is very spare in her arrangement. On the bridge is a wide-open entertainment area with a huge wet bar and a dining table flanked by cushioned bench seats. Below are a master stateroom aft, guest stateroom forward with a large head in the forepeak, and a salon and galley amidships.

Everything is ultra-spacious aboard *Poco Mas*— deckhouse, above; galley, at right; salon, below.

LOA: 74'
Beam: 17'
Draft: 4'6"
Weight: 82,000 pounds, approx., at half load
Fuel: 2800 gallons
Water: 250 gallons
Power: twin 1000-hp G.M. diesels
Hull: Airex-core fiberglass
Designer and builder: Huckins Yacht Corp., Jacksonville, FL

BRIGHT HOUR

Built on the same 74′ Airex-cored hull as *Poco Mas*, *Bright Hour* is a more traditional-looking Huckins, a cruising and fishing machine with virtually the same above-deck profile as two previous Huckins yachts that have taken their owner on fishing forays all over Florida, the Bahamas and the Caribbean.

Owner Calvin Houghland, a Tennessee businessman with Florida interests that include a hotel and a cattle ranch, is an avid sportsman who pursues big game hunting as well as fishing. This *Bright Hour*, the third Huckins with that name, is decorated with trophies and mementoes of hunting and fishing adventures as well as cruises. On one previous *Bright Hour*, Houghland logged 365 days of cruising from Fort Lauderdale to Venezuela and west as far as the Panama Canal. He likes to bring his friends along on these adventures, and the new *Bright Hour* is arranged with two double guest staterooms forward, as well as crew quarters in the forepeak for three. Below the enclosed deckhouse aft is an owner's cabin with queen-sized berth and a head compartment fitted with a tub and Jacuzzi system. Amidships is a big living room of a salon with galley and dinette forward. The pilothouse is fitted with a wet bar and a big padded banquette surrounding a table. At the stern is a low fishing cockpit with three fishing chairs and a big fishbox.

Bright Hour is a big sportfisherman with a flying bridge that looks straight down into the cockpit. On the foredeck is a 13′ Boston Whaler for forays ashore and for thin-water angling. Power is a pair of G.M. 8-92TI diesels from Johnson & Towers, and fuel stowage is 1800 gallons. Top speed is 24.2 knots, and range is 700 nautical miles at a brisk cruising speed of 16 knots. The long-range capabilities of this boat will make her cruising grounds as extensive as those of her predecessors, angling and adventuring in the islands of the Caribbean and along the coasts of Latin America.

NAUTICAL QUARTERLY

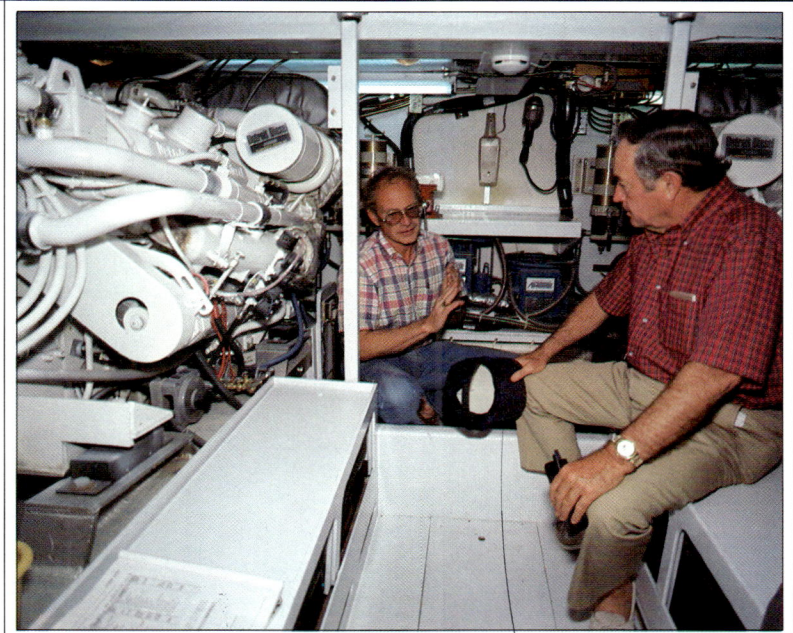

Owner Calvin Houghland discusses his new boat's machinery with Buddy Purcell at right. And at left and below, a few of *Bright Hour*'s spaces—trophy-filled salon, galley, and deck lounge with bar.

LOA: 74'
Beam: 17'4"
Draft: 4'7"
Weight: 82,000 pounds, approx., at half load
Fuel: 1800 gallons
Water: 500 gallons
Power: twin 675-hp G.M. diesels
Hull: Airex-core fiberglass
Designer and builder: Huckins Yacht Corp., 3482 Lakeshore Blvd., Jacksonville, FL 32210

NAUTICAL QUARTERLY

...AND NOT TO YIELD

BY TRISTAN JONES

NAUTICAL QUARTERLY

Heading out to sea again after a seven-year sojourn spent more or less ashore, while easier perhaps for me than for a stark newcomer to ocean sailing, was still not easy. It is as hard to reacquire old habits as it is to discard temporary ones. Bad habits are the most difficult to discard, and "good" habits, being generally thrust upon us, are often our undoing in the long run. □ I had been living boatless for seven years in New York City. There I had hermited myself away in the very middle of that roaring ant heap to work on the nine books I had sworn to myself I would write when I was washed ashore after the long, difficult sailing traipse which I described in the book *The Incredible Voyage*. During these years on the beach, I heeded the sea's call a few times, sliding away from the noise and the game-playing of the city to cruise for short periods with friends in the Baltic, the West Indies and, for one brief week of glory, the Greek Islands. Each time I came back was more painful than the last; but I had work to do and I stuck it out. The Fates at last decided for me, in the form of a leg amputation, that I had had enough of life ashore. It was time to be off again, back to the ocean which gave me life in the first place.

NAUTICAL QUARTERLY

The latest adventures of Tristan Jones have taken him from San Diego to the Panama Canal, through the Caribbean and up to New York, where he arrived in late May. On pages 56-57 he explores a beach in Costa Rica; above, he hosts a party of cruising friends at Cristobal in the Canal Zone; and at near right he visits Captain Tom Claremont's bistro in Golfito, Costa Rica. At far left, Tristan and Wally Rediske inspect the arrangement of running rigging in the cockpit before departure.

> To return to sea in small craft after the shock of losing
> my precious full mobility, together with half of my alimentary tract, at the
> age of close on sixty, is no small thing.

I have to be very careful here. To return to sea in small craft after the shock of losing my precious full mobility, together with half of my alimentary tract, at the age of close on sixty, is no small thing. If it were done by anyone who did not appreciate the risks involved—the isolation from medical assistance, the hazards of moving around in the sometimes violent and rarely steady confines of a sailing vessel, it might be considered more of a stunt than anything else. Even if I did appreciate these things in their full import, and yet had not a lifetime of experience in small ocean-sailing craft, taking up voyaging again would be foolish indeed. But I knew the pitfalls. I knew that I would be exchanging comparitive comfort for the rest of my life, and the ways and means, perhaps, to be creative whilst at ease. I knew that, at least for me, peace of mind—whilst it dwelt on the logistics of a passage, the taunting of wind-direction changes, the teasing of sudden squalls, the holding or not of an anchor (in the making of which I had no part)—would be a rare thing. But I also felt that, when I did have it, peace would be all the more precious.

And so to the story of the beginnings of a voyage around the world—one-legged, single-minded, a challenge singular in every way for me. But first, the story of "my" operation.

I came awake in St. Vincent's Hospital, New York City, after my leg was amputated in March, 1982. One tends to use the personal possessive about an operation—"my" amputation—a bit like my cat or my boat. It came about because some tiny bits of magnesium shrapnel in my left heel bone had shifted somehow into my bloodstream, and were forming a clot. It began when I was in the seaman's district of Amsterdam, knocking back the odd Heineken with the best and worst of them, and soaking in the ambience. Quite suddenly, one fine morning, as I walked along a canal bank, my left hip jolted as if shocked by electricity, and burned, and I could walk no more. My friends carried me to the seaman's clinic, and I found myself in the office of an Indonesian doctor. He took one look at me, in my pea jacket and corduroy pants, hobbling in pain, and pronounced that I had "Zhe Eeengleesh Deezeeze."

"The *what*, Mynheer?" I was not merely concerned now; I was worried.

"Joost a meeneet." The good doctor turned and inspected his bookshelf. He took down an English-Dutch dictionary and consulted it for a minute or two as 20,000 volts stabbed at my left groin. Then he looked up at me and grinned.

"Yes, here eet ees," said he. "...goat."

"Goat, Mynheer?"

"Goot?"

"?"

"Gout?" He asked again.

"Ah yes, *gout*!"

"Ja. Now you not drink more beer. You drink milch and you eat good plain food. Six months—no beer, ja?"

"Ja, Mynheer..." This shakily but sincerely.

And so I did. I returned to my lodging, put my foot up as instructed, and ate only plain food. But the pain became worse and worse, and my left leg turned blue. Three things shatter logical thinking—fear, hunger and pain. And the thing that shatters it most is pain. Real pain engenders despair, and in that way it is worse than fear or hunger. Fear attacks the soul, hunger the body; but pain attacks everything about us. It is our worst enemy in every way except one: it is through pain and, it seems to me, only through pain, that we reach genuine grace. In the most awful agony, in that shabby hotel bedroom in Amsterdam, I made a promise. I am not sure to whom or to what the promise was made, whether to the Power that put the stars on their courses or to my miserable self. I promised that if I should come out of that hell alive I would somehow bend that pain to a good effort, and thus defeat it.

I hardly remember the flight to New York. If I'd had my wits about me I would have gone to London; I could have had free treatment at the Greenwich Seaman's Hospital, an institution renowned for the sagacity and skill of its doctors. But as it was I found myself back in New York at St. Vincent's. New York was where my work was—my books, my typewriter, my little mementos of a lifetime at sea.

I must have looked a real scarecrow, scarcely unlike the others in my ward—some derelicts with frostbitten feet, some "bums" from the Bowery, and a very interesting full-blooded Cherokee Indian who had been smashed with a girder at a height of a hundred and fifty feet above street level. At first, after I awoke minus my old friend my left leg from just below the thigh, the feeling was one of intense relief that the cause of appalling pain was gone. Then, after a moment's reflection, intense anxiety about how I would manage in the future.

After a couple of weeks' vegetation in bed, I was up and about in a wheelchair, and in time getting about the different wards like a racetrack driver. Then I saw and talked with the youngsters, lads and lasses in their teens. They were mostly the victims of car-crashes. Sometimes they held themselves to blame—usually the ones with more "character"—and sometimes not. But in every case they had almost lost hope of ever again being "useful" members of society.

For one of the very rare times in my life, I found myself trying to cheer up people and advise them of circumstances of which I had no experience whatsoever. For my own part, I bitterly resented attempts by some therapists and visitors to mollycoddle me. I resented that—yet I also

> I don't recall consciously thinking of a boat, yet the sense
> that synchronistic fate was guiding me never left me for a moment, until I saw
> the boat lying at anchor off a golf club in San Diego.

resented, almost as much, having to ask someone to do something for me which I could not manage for myself. In the therapy sessions I observed that the most effective therapists were those who were themselves handicapped. Among the patients the most cheerful and hopeful were those who could occupy themselves with some pastime. The least hopeful were those who, in between staring at television, could find no inner resources on which to fall back.

Gradually the seed of an idea, an ambition, grew within me; by the time I left St. Vincent's I was determined to return to sea. But first I would try to show my appreciation of all the messages of encouragement that had arrived for me from readers of my books, and especially from yachtspeople all over the world—more than 5000 letters. I would try to reach them as personally as I could by giving lectures and slide shows. That would kill two birds with one stone; it would help pay a crippling bill of $32,000 for medical expenses. So I went on a lecture tour, flying around as far east as Kiel, Germany, and as far west as Anchorage, Alaska, and all the time in discomfort and sometimes agony with phantom pains, and all the time willing my way back to sea.

There were some good reasons to return to sea. The first was because of what Jack London called "I Like"—just because you bloody well want to. The second, I thought, was to give an example to youngsters ("If that old bugger can do it at 60, then so can I at 18..."). The third was perhaps to chip away at the seeming refusal of "normal" people to treat cripples as if they were rational, sensible human beings. And I think there was yet another reason: to demonstrate that the only way to overcome the sense of hopelessness which is invariably engendered by an amputation is to thrust oneself, or be thrust, back into "normal" activities as swiftly (and, if need be, as brutally) as possible. As the old Victorians amongst whom I was brought up, and who were right in so many little ways, used to say: "Sometimes you have to be a little cruel to be kind." The handicapped should take up, or be made to take up, as soon as possible after their catastrophe, their former activities. They cannot expect to be as proficient as they were formerly, at least not for a longish spell after their renaissance, but they must try.

Reason number five: Ocean sailing by the handicapped is a field of investigation which has so far been hardly touched. Some in the past have made remarkable voyages: Howard Blackburn's crossing of the Atlantic solo in the 1890s with no fingers or thumbs, a Rhodesian couple's crossing of the South Atlantic confined to wheelchairs, another Welshman who sailed from Britain to South Africa solo in a wheelchair. These remarkable things have been done, but not much has been tried in the way of developing new approaches to comfort, safety and security at sea in small vessels for those whose physical abilities are restricted.

It was obvious to me, from the first moment I thought of returning to sea, that I should have to make a completely fresh approach. The first time I ever hobbled onto a sloping sidewalk it was clear that I would find a heeling vessel problematical if not impossible to get around on one leg. It might have worked in the days of big ships under sail with their peg-leg cooks; but in a vessel of around 40', subject to every slight motion of the sea surface, it would be a different matter. It was soon clear that the only kind of vessel which would be suitable was either a catamaran or trimaran. But with both, there was the added problem of the possibility of capsize.

Trimarans seemed to me to offer much more probability of a solution to the capsize hazard—or at least a way to reduce the danger drastically. But the first thing to do was to find a suitable vessel.

Normally, I would not even consider flying right across the United States to give but one lecture and slide show, as the fee would merely cover the expenses. But in this instance, as I sat on my porch in Key West and considered the matter of flying to San Diego, I had that nagging, tremendous feeling that somehow destiny was pushing me. I don't recall consciously thinking of a boat, yet the sense that synchronistic fate was guiding me never left me for a moment, until I saw the boat lying at anchor off a golf club in San Diego. The fact that she was to be the prototype of the Osprey-class trimaran, and that she was to be bought by H&S Bluewater Multihulls and chartered to me for a voyage around the world on very favorable terms did not take me by surprise. It was somewhat, I imagine, like following a film scenario. I first saw the boat we renamed *Outward Leg* on June 29, and we completed the outfitting on October 16. On October 17 we sailed, my young friend Wally Rediske and I, south for the Panama Canal, and eastabout around the world.

In early July I had sailed in the boat—then named *Osprey*—along with her designer, Leo Surtees, and the boss of H&S, Larry Haftl. These were sailing trials off Point Conception, the so-called Cape Horn of the U.S. West Coast. Unloaded, she sailed like a witch on all points. She pointed; she even heaved-to properly; and she tracked as straight as an arrow on a dead downwind run with minimum attention to the wheel. All in all, the trials were a great success, and I managed to get around all three hulls while the boat was underway. It was on these trials that I conceived the idea of what I call "cooltubes." I call my capsize-prevention system this because the thought that they are there, on the keel, makes me feel cool indeed. The idea is that, at the moment of capsize, the fulcrum of capsizing moment is the keel of the leeward outrigger (or ama). If there is a weight below the main hull, the gravitational effect of that weight would be multiplied by the distance of that weight from the fulcrum.

The problem is that in a multihull any kind of unnecessary weight retards performance, and when the boat is not in danger of capsizing a

Outward Leg, with her cooltube ballasting system, probably represents a reduction in the possibilities of a capsize for a multihull to that of a monohull of the same length in the same weather conditions.

weight on the keel of the main hull would be unnecessary. So what was needed was a weight, a mass of ballast, only when it was necessary. This, of course, would be at the moment when the boat's main keel left the water. How to do it?

The only capturable matters at sea are fish, birds, aquatic mammals, air and the sea itself. Therefore, the sea must become the vessel's ballast—but only when needed. Salt water in salt water weighs nothing. So salt water must be the instant ballast. It must be captured so that it is thrusting down when required. So I wrap PVC pipe around it, and close the pipe at both ends. I leave a little hole for a water inlet and another for a water outlet. I wrap copper sheeting inside the PVC pipes to discourage marine growth inside them, and as if by magic I have a capsize prevention device for a trimaran (patent applied for).

As an example of the physics of the thing, two PVC tubes, one each side of the bottom of the keel, each with 6″ outside diameter and 7′ long, will deliver 2104 pounds of downward thrust the moment that the main keel leaves the water. Each tube contains 87.68 pounds of seawater, and the distance from the centerline of each tube to the centerline of each ama is 12′; the weight multiplied by the distance gives us what naval architects call "righting moment." This is a ton of righting moment when needed.

I fully realize that many of the past (and well-publicized) capsizes of multihulls have been caused not by the wind pushing the boat over, but by a rogue sea lifting the vessel and turning her over, and I realize that the keel would tend to remain in the water while this began to happen. But I know—and you know—that frothing water on the top or the leading edge of a rogue wave does not have the same density as solid water, and therefore the ballasting effect of the water in the cooltubes must still impart a downward thrust to the keel. I hope to prove this by testing a model, courtesy of H&S Bluewater Multihulls, and by testing the boat in conditions where a capsize might be expected to occur. So far this has been done in the Gulf of Tehuantepec, a place notorious for the shortness of its troughs and the heights of its seas. We ran very well in winds up to 45 knots, under small staysail alone, before seas about 60′ apart and about 20′ high. I crawled out on one of the amas while this was going on, and observed that, although the main hull was regularly out of the water entirely, not once did the keel emerge. My elation, hanging onto the lower shrouds, was exceeded only by my annoyance as a sea came onboard and filled the top of my false leg with cold water. I found that I had neglected to drill drain holes in it.

Back to the cooltubes. Several knowledgeable and clever heads have already been scratched at the revelation to them of this idea and its application to *Outward Leg.* So far, no one has come up with a logical opposition or objection to it. The simple fact of the matter is that theoretically it must work. And if that is so, then in all probability it will work in practice. What has happened is that *Outward Leg*, with her cooltube ballasting system, probably represents a reduction in the possibilities of capsize for a multihull to that of a monohull of the same length in the same weather conditions.

Now the traditionalists will say "Ah, yes, but a monohull, soundly constructed and well-rigged, will flip right over and return to an upright position, whereas a multihull stays upside-down when she's flipped." To this I reply "Very true, but you missed one little qualifier. You missed the word 'often' between 'flip' and 'right,' and as to multihulls you missed out 'always.'" So, writing as a lifelong "heavy-ballast" man, I say this: If *some* monohulls sink when they capsize, and if *all* multihulls float upside-down, then the multihull, even capsized, must be safer than the monohull when the issue is survival. And if the probability of capsize of the multihull is reduced to that of the monohull of the same length in the same weather, then the multihull must be the all-round safer vessel. Of course, my natural Welsh humility prompts me to point out that I stand to be corrected, and that if I am wrong I shall say so without any apology.

If the capsize bugaboo of multihulls is in the process of being solved once and for all, then I can see only two disadvantages to them:

(1) We shall need more berthing space.

(2) The extent of the deck gives a bigger target for defecating gulls.

It's easy to say I was relieved to depart at last from San Diego after hell-on-wheels outfitting for almost two months—and so, as it's easy, I'm saying it. But life and circumstances are far too complex for anything too easily said to be absolutely true. There had been a great deal of attention to Wally and me and *Outward Leg* from the press and television, and that can be very wearing. Journalists no longer merely report the news—they try to make it happen. They often want to manipulate their subjects into perhaps doing and saying things they think might interest their subscribers, regardless of whether those things are truly said or felt or done. This can be very wearying to resist. Fame should be restricted to people under the age of twenty-one. Otherwise it should be banned by the Surgeon General or someone as being dangerous to one's health.

But when we were done with the journalists our sendoff was heart-stirring, with an escort out of the port of about eight other yachts all crowded with well-wishers, and me trying on the one hand to be blasé about everything, and on the other trying to recall where I'd stowed the damned chart for the first leg.

Courtesy of the Tai-Ping Foundation (which Allah preserve!) a Weatherfax machine had been donated to the project. It worked, too, and as I tested it in San Diego, and watched the miraculous printed weathermap roll off the spool, and listened to the dots and dashes of the

> The harbormaster is a stout gentleman who spends his time
> wafting a kerchief in front of his face under a casuarina tree in the garden outside
> his office a mile and a half away from the harbor.

signals, my eyes misted as I recalled my first dear old skipper, Tansy Lee, onboard the sailing barge *Second Apprentice,* working the North Sea in winter. Tansy's weather-forecasting equipment was a broken old aneroid barometer and a half inch of candle sitting in the bottom of a jam jar. Before sailing he would send Bert, the Mate, along to the end of the jetty or up to the eyes of the boat, and if the wind blew the candle out he would hoist the main with one reef in. The romance of sail!...

After one day and a night in a good northerly breeze, making eight knots, the Weatherfax indicated that hurricane Tico was heading up from Tehuantepec in our direction. Now you might think this was the reason that *Outward Leg* scurried into Ensenada on the afternoon of her second day at sea. Officially it was, but the real reason is much more mundane. We had not yet fitted the head discharge overboard. Now for "normal" people, who can make their way fairly easily to the ship's bow or side, this is no serious matter. But for an "invalid" to do it is an acrobatic exercise, and unless he has no aesthetic feelings at all he must have someone to help him get there, and stay with him until his business is finished. Of course, I couldn't do that, and so we headed into Ensenada to fit a PVC pipe through the wing-deck overhang, into which I could empty the discharge from that most remarkable of maritime inventions—the bucket. Besides, I intended to make the real departure of the voyage from a quieter place than San Diego, so Ensenada it was. We sneaked in, like good cruisers, and sneaked out again. It was a beautiful visit, like cruising used to be in the old days—no questions asked, no answers given, no lies told.

The next stage of the voyage was down south and east, south and east, for sixteen days and nights of sailing mainly off the wind, with the Aries self-steering gear working like a hero, with our twin roller headsails pulling like dray horses. We were reaching speeds of ten knots at times, but mostly, because I suppose of our loaded-down condition, hovering around five knots. Here we found out good and bad points that can only be found out at sea on passage. Our sailing rig is first class—simple and easily handled. Our gear is the best. Our engine is superb. Our food and water stowages are handy and sufficient. The boat is comfortable—more comfortable than any I have ever sailed. But we are electrically underpowered, especially if we are to use the radio very much. I decided to increase our fuel stowage by adding two outside tanks holding thirteen gallons each. And that would be the only weight concession I would make. For the extra weight added, something would have to be landed. I'm still puzzling what that something might be.

Acapulco looked as though it had come off a postcard, at least from the sea. The cheapest things there, fortunately, are the taxi cabs. There are, I was told, seventeen thousand of them in the city. All I needed was two—to get me to and from the Socalo, the old town market place, to see the cathedral and sit in the shade of the trees and watch the world pass by for an hour or two. My mate, Wally, being a very active young man, went walking out around the town, and returned hot and sweaty, whilst I watched him and slowly made up my mind whether to raise my glass of cool limeade with my right or my left hand. Very hot and humid it was.

As we had to buy some fuel in Acapulco, we were more or less constrained into encountering our first—on this trip—Latin bureaucrat. In this we were reminded, after seven years of happy forgetfulness, that the first intent of Latin administration is to make the administrated *wait.* Preferably in hot, fly-blown offices on hard wooden seats. Or, even better, standing on a concrete floor—from whence they can see, through a glass screen, the cool administrators being air conditioned in their crisp white shirt-sleeves. The second function of these ponderous panjandrums, who can be found anywhere the conquistadors set foot, is to prevent anything happening which might benefit the administrated—if it is at all possible. If it is not possible—if, by some wondrous error at some time in the dim past, a gleam of human understanding has chipped a channel through which honest endeavor might somehow trickle into the sunny valleys of goodwill and, however small, achievement—then the third function of Latin bureaucracy is to ensure that the administrated are fully aware of the favors that have been bestowed. This understanding is formalized by exacting tribute—unofficially, of course, and preferably in the form of currency.

In Salinas Cruz, our next port of call, it was the same story; but worse, because this time, besides the port authorities, we had to deal with customs and immigration and with the port's fuel-purchase-prevention officers. A whole book—a manual—could be written about the calvaristic cavalcade which Wally and I went through in Salinas Cruz. As it turned out, it was worth putting in there merely to enjoy the singular elation of leaving the place. At the dead-end of the notorious Gulf of Tehuantepec—and at the dead-end of everything else, come to that—Salinas Cruz is a hot, dirty straggle of half-abandoned structures with tatty tin roofs, inhabited by an unusually unpleasant strain of Mexican. Its harbor water should be worth a fortune to anyone who might extract from it the thick layer of chemical ooze which gently undulates on its surface under the hot sun. The harbormaster is a stout gentleman who spends his time wafting a kerchief in front of his face under a casuarina tree in the garden outside his office a mile and a half away from the harbor. Oh, that mile and a half—that two kilometers of broken pavement and mangy dogs, that Olympic marathon of dust and heat for a one-legged man. How well we know it, every yard, every meter, every foot, Wally and I, after tramping it seven times from the boat, from the immigration office, from the harbor fuel office, from the Federales office, from the Customs office and back, until

Although from the ama the boat seemed to be in torture, back inside the main hull, the movement seemed to be far less, a sort of benevolent wobble, much as felt when riding a kindly camel with a flexible hump.

finally we had in our hot, sweaty fingers the prize, our "zarpe," our permit to sail away from that harbor of Hell.

But perhaps we were unlucky, or we arrived at the quiet time for yachts, or something. Or it may be that I am fated to see things through the eyes of one who knew cruising when the only piece of paper seen was the pound note which no one for ten miles around could change.

Conversation in Salinas Cruz with a Federale policeman, aged about twenty:

Me: "Where are you from?"
"Tehuantepec."
"What did you do there?"
"Nothing."
"Is your family there?"
"Yes." (Fumbles with the catch of his machine pistol).
"What do they do?"
"Nothing."
"Your mother?"
"Yes."
"What does she do?"
"Nothing."
"Your father?"
"Yes."
"What does he do?"
"Nothing."

Our real reason for being in the Gulf of Tehuantepec was to see what would happen to us and how the boat would behave in the steep, short seas which occur when the heavy northerly blows straight down the shallow gulf. Very steep and very short. We headed out right in front of a strong wind blowing straight down from the Sierra Madre and gusting around 30 knots for longish stretches of time. It was late afternoon when we left Salinas Cruz, and we were very soon down to merely the staysail, which is a tiny thing on its own boom. The wind hammered and the sea mounted all night, so that by early morning there was an irregular frenzy all around us and we had been blown south, with the Aries holding us steady, about a hundred miles. I carefully clambered out onto the port ama and, holding on like a fly to a glue-pot, studied the action of the hull, and particularly whether or not the keel was emerging. It was not. The seas by then were about 20 feet high and were no more than eighty feet apart at the most. The boat reared and plunged like a wild thing, but never once did the cooltubes rise above the surface, nor did much of the 4' keel. A surprising thing—or perhaps not—was that, although from the ama the boat seemed to be in torture, back inside the main hull, the movement seemed to be far less, a sort of benevolent wobble, much as felt when riding a kindly camel with a flexible hump.

Towards noon on the second day out of Salinas, still in very heavy seas, a merchant ship changed course to inspect us. She sheered away when I signaled her on the hand-held VHF that I was okay and would continue to be so as long as I could continue to avoid collision with curious merchantmen. The merchant skipper laughed at that and wished us good fortune.

Four hundred miles south of the bloody Gulf of Tehuantepec the calms are encountered—long days of solitary sea, as flat as a baker's tray and as hot. Until the engine won out the waiting game, it was as if God himself were on vacation and there was no one looking after the shop.

I always was curious about Costa Rica. I'd sailed off its coast a few times, and always its geographical setup had intrigued me. Where else can you find a capital city, a microcosm of old Spanish culture, cool and rainy, only a $1.50 bus ride away from a hot, fetid, steamy, humid coast? So we headed into Puntarenas and anchored in the strong tidal stream off the Club Aquatico (all services, fee $1 per day). I took off for San Jose to sit, just once more, under a mountain pine tree in the rain. Away, away, from the heat and the sea—just for one day. And sit there I did, in the rain, while passing peasants on their burros stared at me as though I were mad. The clouds, cool and waterladen, drove in from the south and reminded me of the skies of Wales, so far away.

A quick look around the Opera House of San Jose—worth every minute spent trying to reach it—and then around the big, enclosed public market (where the real opera is played out daily), then back down to the coast on the bus. The only other gringo was a sharp-nosed Frenchman who addressed me in English. I pretended not to understand and replied to him in Welsh. Whereupon he, drat him, replied to me in perfect Irish Gaelic. He had been some sort of lobster wholesaler on the coast of Ireland, it seems, long enough for most of his inborn French obnoxiousness to have worn thin, and so we got along quite well for the rest of the ride. Long enough to sit together on the waterfront parade in Puntarenas, in the cool of the evening onshore breeze. We discussed, among other things, Descartes, and whether the Concorde should have been named Discord.

From Puntarenas our track led to the port of Golfito in the south of Costa Rica. It is a den of thieves. Its only saving graces are a fine view out over the harbor, surrounded by jungle-clad hills, the tiny, privately run yacht club, and Captain Tom Claremont, who was shipwrecked at Cacao Beach, near the harbor entrance, in his ex-sub-chaser, 30-odd years ago, and has been there ever since. Captain Tom, too, is another above the knee leg-amputee, having lost his at the Battle of Guadalcanal in 1943. His jungle burgers are delicious, and his yachtsman's visitors book is four or five volumes of historical record.

Some of the most interesting developments in gear and techniques in modern cruising come from less-well-heeled yachtsmen. And they are some of sailing's most interesting characters.

From Golfito we sailed to Taboga and Balboa, where the yacht club, to anyone who knew it years ago, is but a shadow of its former glory. Paint peels over the litter-strewn stairway to the terrace bar, and the staff hold back studiously from any attempt to assist a visitor, or even to give him much attention, until the time for fee payment and tip-dropping arrives. Mooring fees are exorbitant, and it is demanded that before you can have a mooring buoy to hang onto in oily waters you must become a temporary member of the club. Another $15. My reply to that was a refusal flat and final. I do not wish to be a member of a club where the visitor's telephone is in the noisy and noisome foyer of the toilets, and where moves are afoot to abolish the free anchoring rights for 48 hours in the ground opposite the club moorings on the far side of the ship channel. This is a situation that can lead to only one result: legalized brigandage. Yachts are forced to call at Balboa to be measured for the canal passage. To charge them $15 a night or more, depending on length, for a rolling berth in an oily place only yards from one of the world's busiest shipping lanes is wrong.

That's the bad news—now for the good. The passage through the canal is just as easy as it ever was; the pilots are as helpful; and, best of all, the welcome and friendliness of the staff and members of the Panama Canal Yacht Club in Cristobal is just as warm as it ever was. Unfortunately, the waters around the canal are just as oily, too. But what's a bit of oil? It's the attitude of the people that matters much more, as always.

A summary of our three-legged adventure, then, at the end of its first—excuse the expression—leg:

Miles covered to date: 3898

Days at sea: 32

Strongest wind encountered: 48 knots, Lat. 11.01N, Long. 91.00W, November 15

Highest seas and shortest period: Gulf of Tehuantepec, November 11

Fresh water consumed, San Diego to Panama (two men): 32 gallons

Fastest day's sail: 187 miles (average speed 7.79 knots)

Strongest current encountered: Lat. 09.75N, Long. 88.28W, westerly, three knots

Mishaps: The double roller-headsail masthead block failed twice. The false leg fitted in San Diego is a dismal failure, and caused me to fall five feet down the after companionway. Fifteen new swear words were invented on the spot.

Best port of call: Panama Canal Yacht Club, Cristobal. An alongside berth is provided for me, and fellow ocean-voyagers call regularly onboard to see if there is anything I need while my crew is away.

Worst port of call: Salinas Cruz, Mexico—an oily, inaccessible town and a thriving hive of nefarious officials

Most interesting encounter so far: Captain Tom Claremont, a "castaway" on Cacao Beach, Golfito, Costa Rica

Least interesting encounter: a surly seller of plastic back-scratchers in Acapulco, Mexico. Unusual in that port, even his mutters were derivitive and unoriginal.

Best anchorage: Puntarenas, Costa Rica, although in a two-knot tidal stream. The "Club Aquatico" charges only $1 per day for full services.

Worst anchorage: Isla de Canu, Costa Rica. Smooth rock bottom or boulders around which the anchor rode wraps itself. Never anchor there if you are alone and cannot dive.

Best meal(s): Onboard—all non-refrigerable prepared foods

Worst meal: In a flyblown cafe in Salinas Cruz with a television blaring

Most obvious recent trends on Pacific coasts of Latin America: A rigid and inflexible maintenance—and in many cases an increase—of the traditional obstacle course of immigration and customs. And a disturbing increase in thievery, evidently in direct proportion to the number of television sets in any given locality.

Most interesting political phenomenon: The ability of Costa Rica to maintain a full-blown welfare state, despite the evident paucity of public funds.

Most startling price increase in recent years: maritime charts. This will lead, of course, to a black market in photocopied charts of dubious precision, or to the tracing of charts, and therefore the added possibility of error. This will have tragic navigational consequences for long-distance yachtsmen. The present haphazard agencies for exchanging, buying and selling second-hand charts should be regulated, so that charts are updated each time they change hands. When I first went small-craft voyaging, in 1953, a British Admiralty chart cost about one dollar. Now the average price is twelve dollars. It is no good for the richer people among us to observe that if one cannot afford it one should not undertake long voyages. Some of the most interesting developments in gear and techniques in modern cruising come from less-well-heeled yachtsmen. And they are some of sailing's most interesting characters. It will be a great loss to ocean sailing when comparatively poor youngsters cannot find some way to head out against the Great Challenge. It will be a loss to us all.

Editor's Note: We will publish a second installment of Tristan Jones's adventures in the next issue, with details of *Outward Leg*'s visit to the lawless and infamous Caribbean coast of Colombia. Tristan's circumnavigation is expected to take him from New York to England this summer, followed by a cruise in the Baltic in late summer. In the fall, he plans to transit the German inland waterway system and bring *Outward Leg* all the way to Budapest; from there he will cruise down the Danube to the Black Sea and investigate the yachting scene on the Russian Riviera.

YES, MR. LOOMIS, THERE ARE SOME SAILORS IN THE NAVY

BY A.B.F. FRASER-HARRIS

Alfred Loomis, alias "Spun Yarn," asked a question in a 1932 article in Yachting which he titled "Are There Any Sailors in the Navy?" Loomis questioned the qualifications of naval officers in basic seamanship, and wondered why the yachtsmen of America were not, as were their British and European counterparts, being challenged by their own Navy in offshore races. This pot-stirring got swift reaction. ☐ The United States Naval Institute magazine, Proceedings, published a number of letters both supporting Loomis and defending the Navy. One anonymous letter backed up Yachting's great gadfly and sage by stating: "In spite of the efforts of many naval officers interested in sailing, there is a most inadequate outfit of small sailing craft at Annapolis which midshipmen who might desire to become proficient in handling boats under sail can use, and no effort is being made to get the future officers of our Navy interested in small-boat seamanship." Loomis had lamented that the Navy, by not taking part in ocean racing, was losing an opportunity to give its men an intimate knowledge of the sea. Is it significant that his supporter should have been anonymous? Does it suggest that his words might have been heresy, damaging to a career? The letter ends with the story of a big-ship captain who has just brought his battered vessel into port after spending eighty hours on the bridge, and comments upon those in the shore establishments: "...they all sit there and draw up specifications. Handling a ship is just a matter of mechanics. Put more gadgets aboard. Every contingency allowed for, though it seems to me there is always one thing they leave out. About the most important thing, too, if you ask me. But I ain't never seen it in a specification yet. What's that? Something you don't get out of books! Something there ain't any button for! Something maybe you don't need from one year's end to another, but when you do need it, you need it damned bad! Seamanship."

The Naval Academy's sailing programs operate on two fronts: big-boat sailing on the famous Luders-designed yawls, shown in downwind action at left, and on cruising and racing yachts donated by yachtsmen, and small-boat activity in several fleets of one-designs such as the Lasers shown here. The first of the original wooden "Naval Academy yawls" were delivered in 1939, and fiberglass replacements to the same design were commissioned by the Navy in 1963 and 1964. They have formed the backbone of the training fleet, and have served as vehicles for intercollegiate competition, for a generation. Donated yachts, now accepted as tax-deductible charitable contributions by the Naval Academy Sailing Foundation, incorporated in 1973, have amounted to some 80 vessels, large and small, since Vamarie was given to the Academy in 1936.

An interesting contrary opinion came from Lieutenant W.S.G. Davis, U.S.N. Far from remaining anonymous, Lt. Davis followed the great naval custom of proving his point by quoting a famous admiral. He tells of Rear Admiral Wat Tyler Cluverius (with a name like that, he had to be good for a quote) who had, upon assuming the duties of Commandant of the Great Lakes Training Center after forty years in the service, told the story of *his* predecessor, whose first act had been to order his men to fill the boat breakers with drinking water. He had forgotten he was sailing upon fresh water. Admiral Cluverius would not, he said, make the same mistake. He praised the men he found at his new command saying, "Our best recruits come from the Middle West, but we have a tough time teaching them to swim in salt water. Furthermore, the Navy does not want seamen. We need the type of mind suitable for mechanics. That's what the Navy is today, and we find it most frequently in the boys from the Middle West."

The Lieutenant, having enlisted the support of this elderly prophet, goes on: "In other words, the Navy, like the world in general, has progressed far beyond the age of sail—we are in the age of machinery, and are passing into that of electricity. Our modern ships are turbo-electric drive, those of the Germans diesel drive, and it appears that before long one will pass into the age of diesel-electric drive. Therefore, it is not sailors, but mechanics that are the Navy's crying need, as Admiral Cluverius has so clearly stated."

This divergence of opinion concerning sail and seamanship training in a modern Navy has been alive for a century. And, as seems true with most controversy, the answer probably lies somewhere in the middle. It also lies, characteristically, in a muddle—of history, of technology, of personality. The mission of the Naval Academy, established in Annapolis in 1845, under the command of Captain George Bancroft, was stated specifically as being "to train naval officers for a steam navy." A century later, Admiral Rickover was to switch the emphasis from steam to nuclear. The mechanic was now to become a physicist. Is there time or place in four years of demanding study and athletics at the Naval Academy for basic seamanship and sail training?

There has, since Alf Loomis's time, been a considerable increase in sailing activity at the Academy, but it would be foolhardy to assume that today's naval educators admit to an increased requirement for seamanship training under sail. Midshipmen now take part in many ocean races, and stand high in intercollegiate competition at all levels, but the fact that there are now sailors in the Navy has not been an accident. The improvement has been the result of continuing efforts on the part of dedicated yachtsmen and individual naval enthusiasts who frequently have had to fight established naval doctrines to gain their objectives.

However, it is very encouraging to see that there has recently been an official recognition of "sailing" at the Academy. The post of Director of Sail Training was created in 1980 and assigned to Commander John Bonds. His function is the coordination of both instructional and recreational sailing throughout the fleets and shore establishments. He has since been promoted to Captain and has, this year, been elected a lifetime honorary member of Britain's Royal Naval Sailing Association—a significant honor

The current Naval Academy fleet consists of about 12 donated Class A yachts, the ocean-training ketch *Astral*, a dozen of the fiberglass Luders yawls, six Shields sloops, 30 420 dinghies, 24 Lasers, 30 Rainbow knockabout sloops, and a number of sailboards which were recently acquired. This may seem an adequate fleet; but it must serve 4000 candidates for instruction during a given year, plus intercollegiate racing events, ocean-racing activity, and the annual summer offshore cruises now undertaken.

> The Academy's midshipmen get excellent technical training
> and develop great physical fitness, but they do not get their hands dirty
> and no emphasis is placed upon practical training.

and one not given casually. The United States and British Navies now share the belief that there *is* a place within a modern and highly technical seagoing service for sailing, both for training and recreation.

It is probably easier to appreciate the use of sailing as a professional training aid for a seagoing career when the issue is not clouded by the contiguous matter of ship propulsion, now ancient history. Officers of a modern navy certainly require sophisticated technical training; on the other hand, bookworms are not necessarily effective at sea. Naval officers come into daily contact with many members of other seagoing professions, both at home and abroad. It is important that they possess at least sufficient grounding in practical seamanship and an understanding of the element on, under, or over which they operate to deal intelligently with their nautical brethren. To the merchant seaman, fisherman, port captain, pilot, harbormaster or yachtsman, the man dressed in blue and gold who neither understands the language nor knows how to conduct himself aboard vessels large or small will command little respect. On foreign duty, even in the most obscure places, the yacht club is a preferable meeting place to the local bar.

The Academy's midshipmen get excellent technical training and develop great physical fitness, but they do not get their hands dirty and no emphasis is placed upon practical training. This latter is a national rather than a naval phenomenon; it is common in industry, where the young graduate goes directly into an office, rarely spending time on the shop floor. True, the midshipmen do a number of training cruises during their summers; but the experiences are not always profitable; they tend to go as onlookers rather than participants, or so I am told by those who have recently undergone these exercises. When the midshipman finally goes to sea as an Ensign and is, for instance, appointed as "Boat Officer," he does not drive the boat. He stands around "in charge" giving orders.

The U.S. Navy, recognizing that in this age of technical sophistication it is impossible for a man to be a Jack of all trades, is now moving towards the more common international practice of separating the engineer from the deck officer in ships at sea. It is perhaps timely to suggest that those destined for "driving" (ship, submarine or aircraft) might devote more time to seamanship and sail-training while at the Academy, while those choosing an engineering career might profitably undertake some practical mechanical, electrical and electronic training, the better to supervise and instruct those who will later be under them. And whatever the specialization, a young man or woman joining the Navy should enjoy messing about in boats, and should be encouraged in this enthusiasm on general principles. Was Loomis right? What has been going on in recent years since he dropped his bombs on naval targets?

During the latter half of the last century and early in this one, sail training was still carried out in "school ships" such as *Severn*, in which midshipmen went to sea for short cruises. There was also recreational sailing at the Academy, but not much. In 1895, the yacht *Medusa*, later renamed *Robert Center*, was presented to the Navy by Mrs. Mary E. Ludlow as a memorial to her son, Robert Center, who had been killed by falling from the topmast of a sail-training ship while trying to "spike his cap" to the truck. This was a very noble gesture, and perhaps characteristic of its time. Were the unhappy accident to occur in today's litigious society, one fears that a more probable reaction would be a mother's complaint to her Congressman and, under the guidance of a lawyer on contingency, a suit against all concerned.

Safety is very properly emphasized in current sail-training and racing programs. Partially this is because those concerned are fearful that a fatal or serious accident would jeopardize the whole scheme of sail training. In preparing young men and women as leaders in a combat service, however, a disproportionate anxiety that someone is going to get hurt is inappropriate. Sail training is "safer" today, however, than in my own youth when six young midshipmen (aged 17) were dispatched in a ship's whaler from the cruiser *H.M.S. Achilles* in Barbados and told to rendezvous in St. Lucia three days later. It was an easy downhill sail, and the whaler was a fine seaboat; but one remembers waves as small mountains that had to be climbed and the horizon as very far away. I doubt that our safety was of great concern; we were simply expected to be there. It was, after all, a part of our training as young officers preparing to live and work upon the sea. The only setback experienced was an evil smell on day two which, after we had regarded each other for some time in silent suspicion, was finally traced to a couple of flying fish which had come aboard during the night and were discovered concealed and congealed beneath the floorboards.

Many yachts have been presented to the U.S. Navy since *Medusa*. Hundreds of civilians have contributed to the training of midshipmen under sail. They act as race committee, safety officers, coaches and lecturers. The ladies oversee the provisioning of the yachts for ocean passages. Liaison between the Naval Academy Sailing Squadron and Annapolitan yachtsmen is outstanding. Historically, this cooperation may be attributed in some measure to Captain L. N. McNair, a supporter of Loomis, who wrote in 1933: "Isn't it a fact that in our efforts to master these complicated fighting machines entrusted to our care, we have developed a breed of naval officer that is more of a highly trained technician than he is a sailor—that pressed for time, and fitting himself to do his present-day work, he has slowly drawn away from the salty side of his calling and is spending all his hours with his guns and his gadgets? Necessary you may say, to keep up with the game—but I cannot agree

> By 1933, Marconi-rigged knockabouts were augmenting the gaff-rigged sloops known as "Half-raters" that had been providing small-boat training. In 1924, four Star-class yachts had been added to the fleet.

with you. Furthermore, it appears a shame not only from a personal point of view, but from a professional as well. In the first place, this new naval officer is missing a patch of fun and excitement, in the second he is neglecting a course in the best possible school for ship-handling, and in the last place denying himself association with the finest and best of sportsmen—the yachtsmen the world over." After discussing the merits of small-boat sailing as a training aid for "lads from inland homes far removed from the water" (our Midwest mechanics!) he went on to say, "Now a word as to our friend the yachtsman. Do you think that we can swing the yachting fraternity in behind the Navy with a wholehearted spirit of cooperation and understanding necessary to be of any real benefit to the Navy in peace or war? I don't believe we can do it unless we know his stuff, do it well, and speak his language. The only way to do it is to shift into sailing togs and go to it, and it's a great game."

During the first two decades of this century some progress was made in sail training at the Academy. *Robert Center* (ex *Medusa*) was being sailed by the midshipmen, although correspondence suggests that she was hardly fully employed. She appears to have been used mainly for social sailing. Her demise almost has a humorous touch, although somewhat macabre. In 1932, after some debate as to her further economic employment, she was surveyed. The report contains the following remarkable paragraph: The Board found the *Robert Center* "*in good condition as to cleanliness and in satisfactory condition as to preservation* except that the rudder is missing, the overhang of the stern is in poor condition, rudder post and housing are in poor condition, bulwarks are in poor to fair condition and portions of the framing and planking are rotting..."

One wonders what was left to be satisfactory. And one must be glad that she was clean! She was sold. By 1933, Marconi-rigged knockabouts were augmenting the gaff-rigged sloops known as "Half-raters" that had been providing small-boat sail training. In 1924, four Star-class yachts had been added to the fleet to give the midshipmen some experience in yachts with higher performance. It is significant that when Bob McNitt, a midshipman who joined the Academy in 1935 and is now a retired Rear Admiral and Dean of Admissions, first saw these Stars, he found them "chocked up ashore, their bottoms painted with red lead, and what rigging there was, 'clothesline.'"

Rear Admiral David Sellers, appointed Superintendent in 1934, was the first "Supe" to become actively involved in the promotion of sailing. He not only believed in the value of sail training, but was prepared to put his career on the line for its improvement. Obviously he inspired a number of midshipmen with the same fervor. David Seaman, later to retire and become a prominent yachtsman and businessman, was Commodore of the Midshipman's Boat Club; Bob McWethy, retired Captain and currently Secretary of the United States Naval Sailing Association, a man who has devoted his retirement to working with the midshipmen as head of the race committee and offshore coach; and Bob McNitt, who still plugs Navy sailing, were all there at the same time. Seaman and McNitt petitioned the Superintendent to provide some suitable boats to the midshipmen in the late 1930s. The Admiral responded, and funds were provided for the conversion of four large motor cutters in the Norfolk shipyard. These strange beasts, rigged with auxiliary sail, and appropriately christened *Bullfrog*, *Turtle*, *Crocodile* and *Alligator*, were duly collected from Norfolk by midshipmen crews under Seaman's command. In the words of McWethy, "they didn't sail worth a damn, but provided wonderful 'drag parties,'" thus fulfilling their allotted task of creating the opportunity for midshipmen to enjoy themselves upon the water.

On November 11, 1936, the yacht *Vamarie* was presented to The Brigade of Midshipmen at a ceremonial dress parade by her owners, Vadim and Marie Makaroff. Unbelievably, as if Seaman in the role of Commodore of the midshipmen's sailing activities wasn't name enough, the Brigade Commander who accepted the yacht from Mrs. Makaroff was Midshipman R. B. Woodhull! *Vamarie* was a beautiful wishbone ketch, built to Makaroff's specifications and to the designs of Cox & Stephens of New York by Abeking & Rasmussen at Bremen. Launched in 1933, she was at the time of her presentation virtually a new vessel.

Vadim Makaroff was the son of a Russian admiral who had died at the battle of Port Arthur during the Russo-Japanese war; he had held the rank of Captain in the Imperial Russian Navy before fleeing the Revolution to become a naturalized American citizen. Shortly after the presentation, President Roosevelt received a telegram suggesting that this gift from "the son of a cossack of the sea" could be seen as "suggestive and odious propaganda." Roosevelt was both a sailor and too big a man to defer to such rubbish; Admiral Sellers, however, had to go to a great deal of trouble to establish the identity and motive of the sender of the telegram, and was required to write various reports in justification of *Vamarie*.

It is, of course, valid at this point to observe that obtaining money through service channels for the support of sail training was greatly complicated by the misconception that anything to do with yachting connoted some vain involvement with "a rich man's toy."

Shortly after *Vamarie's* acquisition, Loomis fired another broadside, this time writing as "Spun Yarn" in the August, 1935, issue of Yachting:

"I'm the guy, they tell me, who prompted Bill Makaroff to donate *Vamarie* to the Navy and, if I am that important, I have another suggestion to make. When I tootled into Annapolis the other day in a motor boat, I looked her over with a paternal interest which at once developed into a nausea. The sheen is gone from her lovely

Some snapshots from the Academy's archives show sail-training activity from the past: the *USS Chesapeake* in 1901, above; seamanship drill in cat-rigged half-raters at about the same time, center; and the lovely *Vamarie*. The first yacht donated to the Academy, *Vamarie* was designed by Cox & Stephens and built in Germany by Abeking & Rasmussen in 1933.

mahogany topsides, green grass grows below her boot-top, and the inserted plank in her port side which repairs the damage done to her after she went aground on Greenbury Point looks like the trademark of a wood butcher. In short, she looks as though she had been neglected for two years—whereas the Navy has had her in its tender care for less than eight months. 'Are there any sailors in the Navy?' That's old hat, and the question now is: Will someone give the Navy five gallons of varnish and find out how much red tape has to be cut before a civilian can be put aboard her to make her look like a yacht again?"

Vamarie raced in an event from Gibson Island to Annapolis and finished sixth in a fleet of twenty seven. That's coming down in the world for a lady that used to be cared for like one who was accustomed to leading the way."

Correspondence in the archives reveals that Makaroff had hoped that his Sailing Master would remain on board to look after the vessel. This was not to be, since his salary of some $250 a month plus keep was considered to be beyond the naval purse. The results of this parsimony were, in the long run, to prove disastrous.

The unfortunately common attitude of many naval officers at that time is clearly demonstrated by the following memo, which was written by the Commandant of Midshipmen in reply to a request from Captain J.F. Shafroth, then commanding the base ship *Reina Mercedes,* suggesting that *Vamarie* should be entered in the 1938 Bermuda race: "…The only requirement for amateurs in all these races is that the owner and navigator must be amateurs, and it will be found that those engaged in racing, even including the afterguard, are pretty rough characters. Apparently ocean racing bears no more resemblance to small-boat racing than does intramural boxing compare with heavyweight championships."

This was the man responsible for overseeing midshipman training! One wonders what had happened to the maxim which served us as the basis for sound officer training, "…the gentlemen shall learn to haul and draw with the mariners." He and the Superintendent must have been somewhat at loggerheads. Perhaps because the former was also the senior, perhaps because the midshipmen themselves had not been idle, this cantankerous Commandant went down to defeat. Midshipmen Seamen and McNitt were lobbying among their yachting connections. McNitt wrote a letter (contents undisclosed) to Senator Walsh, a family sailing acquaintance. Not long thereafter, Lewis Compton, Assistant to the Secretary of the Navy, "happened" to visit the Academy. During his tour he was piped aboard *Vamarie* and made aware of her attributes. David Sellers undoubtedly turned "Nelson's blind eye" to these subtle deviations from official channels. The cause was upheld and *Vamarie* did race to Bermuda in '38. The Navy had made it—sort of. She did not do very well, finishing 29th out of 44 in a race she should have won. Cox & Stephens had suggested that she should have aboard an experienced racing man as an

> As American participation in WWII approached, Navy sailors could look back with some pride on the considerable expansion their activities had enjoyed in the 1930s with the aid of the yachting community.

advisor, but this had not been heeded. In the same year a squad of midshipmen which included Bob McNitt took the four Star boats on their European training cruise. They first raced the British cadets from *H.M.S. Britannia* on the River Dart, using the old 14′ wooden dinghies they sailed at that establishment, and beat them. Unfortunately they were subsequently defeated by German officers racing at Kiel, in Stars.

Perhaps the greatest triumph, certainly for the long haul, was the ability of Admiral Sellers to persuade BUSHIPS to provide funds for the construction of 12 wooden Luders-designed yawls for the use of midshipmen in training and competition. The first of these, *Alert, Intrepid* and *Resolute*, were delivered in 1939 and were to form the backbone of the training fleet. Their fiberglass replacements, which came along in 1963 and 1964, still provide enormous impetus to the Academy's intercollegiate competitions, and they have proved to be excellent training yachts.

At a presentation ceremony on September 13, 1940, Mr. Stirling Morton donated the 62′ schooner *Freedom*, and shortly before this the cutter *Highland Light* was bequeathed to the Navy in the will of Mr. Dudley Wolfe, together with a substantial grant in aid for her maintenance. The Navy also added twelve International 14 dinghies. By the end of the 1940 season, *Highland Light*, skippered by Commander Clark Withers, head sailing coach, with a crew of midshipmen, had won the Cruising Division trophy of the Chesapeake Bay Yacht Racing Association two years in succession. As American participation in WWII approached, Navy sailors could look back with some pride on the considerable expansion their activities had enjoyed in the 1930s with the aid of the yachting community.

During the war years, yachtsmen in their hundreds joined the Allied fleets and manned the "small-ship" navies. Many became commanding officers almost overnight, and brilliant although not always "regulation" performances were turned in, contributing much to the Allied victory at sea. There was a saying in the British Royal Navy that, whereas naval officers were gentlemen, but not always seamen, and Merchant Navy officers were seamen but not always gentlemen, the Wavy Navy (Volunteer Reserves so called because they wore wavy stripes), who were mostly yachtsmen, were usually both. A story that would not have amused our stuffy Commandant. Nor would he have appreciated the old yachting dictum that the three most useless things to take aboard a yacht were a rake, a garden mower and a naval officer.

The Naval Academy crew of *Royono* gathers in the cockpit for a portrait in the early 1950s. At the helm is Lt./Cdr. Frank Siatowski, with Navy sailing coach Captain Warren Boles behind him. Designed by John Alden and built by the Herreshoff Manufacturing Company, the 72′ yawl was presented to the Academy in 1950 by John B. Ford, Jr., and she wrote a glorious chapter of Naval Academy sailing history under Frank Siatowski's command. Alf Loomis himself was aboard in 1950 when she placed second to John Nicholas Brown's *Bolero* in the Bermuda race with a crew of midshipmen. In 1952 she won the biennial Newport-to-Bermuda test. Frank Siatowski served as the Academy's "Sailing Master" from 1948 until his retirement in 1956. Siatowski was a genuine old salt, an experienced yachting professional who rapidly gained both the respect and the affection of the midshipmen. But his tenure was not without its problems. The Navy was unwilling to promote him, claiming he was too old, and several yachtsmen were offering him more money and less work as a yacht captain. Thanks to heavy lobbying on the part of the Academy's Superintendant, Siatowski was finally promoted to Lieutenant Commander and one more crisis in the history of the Academy's sailing program was resolved.

The years after the war saw an intensification of effort to safeguard the position of sailing at the Academy. In 1945 a committee was set up to establish ground rules for the supervision of sail training. Lieutenant-Commander J. D. Higgins was appointed as "Sailing Officer" and chairman of a liaison committee. He was directed to work closely with the Commanding Officer of the base ship *Reina Mercedes* concerning maintenance, with the Executive Department regarding scheduling and crew assignments, with the Department of Seamanship and Navigation Training on the subjects of training and qualification, and finally with the Naval Academy Athletic Association for arrangements of intercollegiate events. This officer had indeed to be a juggler of great skill to sort out that lot and keep all the balls in the air. *Vamarie* and *Highland Light* were entered in the Bermuda Race in 1946, and Sherman Hoyt, naval reservist and yachtsman, returned to active duty to train their crews, plus those of two yawls, *Lively* and *Resolute*, for the '48 race. Perhaps events were now moving too fast. Certainly not everything was as it should have been.

Maintenance facilities remained deficient; there was (as there is today) a shortage of personnel trained in yacht maintenance, which differs profoundly from work done on the "grey funnel" ships. In a very damning report, Hoyt complained about the shabby appearance of the boats. He was highly critical, warranting that the standard of joinery was acceptable only for farmyard chicken houses.

This time the rescue squad was headed by John Nicholas Brown, then serving his country as Assistant Secretary of the Navy for Air. He enlisted the support of Admiral J. L. Holloway, concurrently Superintendent of the Naval Academy (later Chief of Naval Operations). Both were sailors and talked the same language. Once again we see two competent men sorting out a mess that had developed because an insufficiently high standard of seamanship and ship husbandry existed in the general ranks of the Navy. It was the old story of trying to fill a leaky bucket. From this meeting sprang a committee of yachtsmen who would be available to advise the Superintendent concerning sail training at the Academy. DeCoursey Fales,

The years after the war saw an intensification of effort to safeguard the position of sailing at the Academy. In 1945 a committee was set up to establish ground rules for the supervision of sail training.

Carleton Mitchell and Bob Bavier were among the first to volunteer. Carleton remembers that Sherman Hoyt, who was not a member, did most of the work. Thus began a long-term association between yachtsmen and the Academy. Several times revived and reorganized during the intervening years, and now known as the Fales Committee, this body is very much alive today and involves some 15 people, plus a number of associate members who look after the Naval Academy Sailing Foundation. This is a team that reflects great credit upon the United States yachting community. The Secretary of this committee was to be the Captain of the base ship *Reina Mercedes*, and when this vessel was scrapped in 1957 the appointment changed to Commanding Officer of the Navy Base.

As the "small-craft" maintenance facility was located in this base, and its C.O. was also *ipso facto* Commodore of the Naval Academy Sailing Squadron, which had been first formed for the officers and faculty but was now becoming the focal point for all sailing at the Academy, this came near to the Committee's recommendation that one officer should be responsible for all sailing activity at the Academy. The idea was good, but this appointment carried with it all the affairs of a Navy Base which was also a Fleet Barracks. However keen a sailor the appointee might be, he had a great deal more on his slop-chit than simply organizing the sailing; moreover, as he is rotated every two years, continuity and long-term planning was and is adversely affected.

Additionally, in 1948, a "Sailing Master" at the Academy was appointed. At last the Navy was on the right track. In Lieutenant Frank Siatowski they had found a genuine old salt, a sailor who rapidly gained both the affection and respect of the midshipmen. He remained at the Academy until his retirement in 1956, but his tenure was not without problems. The Navy was unwilling to promote him, claiming he was too old, and several yachtsmen were offering him more money and less work as a private skipper. Thanks to heavy lobbying on the part of the Superintendent he was, however, finally promoted to Lieutenant-Commander and the crisis passed.

On April 13, 1950, John B. Ford, Jr. presented to the Academy the 72' yawl *Royono*, designed by John Alden and built by Herreshoff. In the same year the contest for the McMillan Cup, the oldest intercollegiate big-boat race, which had until then been raced in borrowed boats in the Marblehead area, was moved to Annapolis and raced in the yawls.

Five years before, 30 Tempest dinghies had been provided by the Navy to the Academy's growing fleet. Thus, with the yawls, the Navy was at last in a position to repay some of the debt owing to the civilian yachtsmen. The Academy began to host a number of intercollegiate events. A brief history of the McMillan Cup is worthwhile. In 1929, Princeton had for the third time won the Oliver May Trophy, presented for a three-way regatta among Princeton, Harvard and Yale. This retired the cup, and a group of Princeton sailors came up with the idea of presenting a new trophy, this time for any East Coast university or college which could produce a suitable crew. William McMillan, at that time a graduate student at Princeton, had just sold his Alden yawl *Merry Widow,* and so, even in the fateful year of 1929, had enough cash on hand to have the cup designed to his specification by Tiffany and also replace his yacht with another Alden yawl. Being a modest man, he stipulated that his name should not appear on the cup, and it does not; however, the McMillan Cup it became and remains to this day. The thrill of racing large class boats around the buoys makes it a very popular event for the young sailors.

Later, after the death of President Kennedy, a number of his friends were to get together and present the Kennedy Cup. This time the competition was to be between universities and colleges chosen on a regional basis from all corners of the United States. This, too, is raced in the yawls, and is the opening event in the spring, while the McMillan cup closes the season.

The Navy even turned the other cheek to Alf Loomis, for he was invited aboard *Royono* for the 1950 Bermuda race in which she acquitted herself well, placing second to John Nicholas Brown's *Bolero*. In '52 *Royono*, under the command of Frank Siatowski, won the Bermuda race. Could it be that the Navy had vindicated itself? Indeed, it seemed so. Unfortunately, an old pattern seems to have been repeated. Changes of personnel brought about changes of fortune. In 1954, during hurricane Hazel, *Vamarie,* which had been left at a mooring on a single bridle, snapped the chain. There were crew aboard, and they attempted to anchor; a tug was sent to her assistance, but the tug fouled its screw in her anchor rode and both vessels were swept down onto the seawall. *Vamarie* was declared a total loss. One must feel that had a professional skipper been aboard he would never have allowed this vessel to face a hurricane threat on a single bridle at a mooring. Thus resulted a sad and serious loss, in addition to a damaging blow to Navy prestige. It was a story of spoiling the ship for a halfpenny's worth of tar, with a vengeance. In 1956, two Academy yawls, *Fearless* and *Resolute,* collided off Hackett's Point and the latter sank. She was refloated and repaired, but coming so soon after the *Vamarie* disaster further damage was done to the Academy's reputation.

It was not so much these unhappy incidents which formed the basis for serious criticism, but the questionable standard of maintenance. This time it was Bunny Rigg, well-known yachting correspondent, Editor of Skipper, and another writer not given to mincing words, who lit into BUSHIPS for their parsimony. In the same article in Skipper, Rigg criticized the policy of rotating personnel as soon as they were suitably

> By 1964, the tide turned yet again. *Freedom*, the old schooner still with the Academy, along with *Royono*, represented the U.S.N.A. in the first Operation Sail in New York.

trained to repair the yachts. He concluded that "the rotation of personnel at 'Small Craft,' and lack of funds from BUSHIPS, provide such poor maintenance facilities that, if nothing is done, the midshipmen will be reduced to sailing dinghies." He called this "a national disgrace."

After Siakowski's retirement in '56 it seems there was a period when no one was at the helm. Documents in the archives reveal that by 1961 complaints were mounting. "There were too many varsity letters being awarded for sailing." "Overnight sails were mere 'boondoggles.'" "The Navy had more boats than it could handle," etc. Once more the Fales Committee was called upon for help. They came up with a number of recommendations, and again a marked improvement in the fortunes of Academy sailing resulted.

One recommendation was for a full-time naval officer to be responsible for sail training, and another was that the Midshipman's Boat Club should be disbanded. By 1964, the tide turned yet again. *Freedom*, the old schooner still with the Academy, along with *Royono*, represented the U.S.N.A. in the first Operation Sail in New York. Bob McNitt, now a Captain, was in command of *Royono*. They did a fine job, and in the same year *Fearless*, with Lieutenant Wallace Tobin as skipper, "rolled down to Rio" for the Buenos Aires to Rio Race. A local comment upon this occasion was, "This group of fine young men taking part in a foreign race on *Fearless* was contributing a great deal more to furthering cordial foreign relations than a bevy of striped pants diplomats." There must, however, have been times when Fales Committee members despaired of getting Navy sailing up to required standards; for again, in 1966, Senator Saltonstall, himself a keen yachtsman, was heard to comment upon the unseamanlike appearance and performance of Academy boats. This continuing swing of the pendulum of competence within Academy sailing indicates the slender thread by which the art of seamanship and boatkeeping remained attached to the Navy as a whole. The "mechanics" just didn't seem too good at spit and polish, or attention to detail, which is synonymous. Today, it is not impossible for officers and midshipmen alike to pass by an Admiral's Flag and a National Ensign improperly hoisted on slack halyards. A year or so ago, the Y.P. training vessels passed in review at the June Week celebrations with fenders over the side, and no one seemed concerned or appeared to notice.

With the appointment of Rear Admiral Draper Kauffman as Superintendent in 1965, we see the beginning of a more permanent base for sailing activities. Admiral Kauffman worked closely with the Fales Committee, whose membership now included many famous names—Henry Anderson; Cornelius Shields, who had presented six of his wonderful sloops to the Academy; Clayton Ewing and Charles Ill from the Eastern Shore, great yachtsmen both; Robert C. Allan from the West Coast, member of the Olympic Committee…The list was virtually a "Who's Who" of the yachting world.

Kauffman even succeeded, in 1966, in arranging to have Captain Jacob J. Vandergrift appointed to command of the Navy Base. Specially selected for his sailing ability, Vandergrift was the right man to put sailing at the Academy firmly on an even keel. His wife set the tone for his administration by arriving from Boston in command of the family yawl. Tragically, this comparatively young officer died of a heart attack in 1969 while still in the appointment; but he had already gone a long way in establishing a permanent organization for the sailing program. One of his earliest accomplishments was to engage Doris Snyder as the first permanent appointee to the position of Civilian Secretary to the Academy Sailing Squadron. Doris, who is still "Anchor Lady" at the Crown Center and "Den Mother" to the sailing midshipmen, was a happy choice. Before coming to the Academy she had been Director of the Washington Redskinettes, a football cheerleading squad! Vandergrift, spotting this on her record, had decided that if she was tough enough to chase 38 girls around a football field, she could probably cope with the mids. She could, she has, and she still does! Above all, she supplies some of that most wanted commodity in the sailing program—continuity.

Another boost to the program came from an unlikely beginning. "Ill blows the wind that profits nobody." The Vietnamese war had begun, and in a number of boot camps and Officer Candidate Schools throughout the country were young sailors well known to the Fales Committee members. These men were the new generation of skilled sailors, some of Olympic standard, and it was recognized that their skills would be best employed teaching sailing and repairing yachts at the Naval Academy.

Doris Snyder remembers the fantastic enthusiasm of these young men, both commissioned and non-commissioned, their skill as instructors, and the tremendous spirit they engendered in the whole program. One of them, Scott Allan, now boss of Horizon Sails and son of Fales member Robert Allan, recalls wondering why funds for the support of the sailing program were so hard to come by when it was obvious that the poor standard of shiphandling in the Navy was proving very expensive! He quoted the example of two submarines which were sent up the Chesapeake to give midshipmen familiarization training in submarines. In the space of a week, not only did they succeed in colliding with each other, but one, docking, ran headlong into the wall, hitting it so hard it bent her bow like a broken nose. He reckoned that the cost of these incidents alone would have paid the Academy's sailing bill for a year or more. This generation of instructors did a sterling job, and many of the young midshipmen whom they trained in those war years went on to become top competitive sailors.

Back in the 'fifties it had been decided that the Intercollegiate Sailing

> Yachts come from all sources, a famous later arrival being *Insurgence*. Her name does not appear on the donors' list, for she came via the courts, having been confiscated as a drug runner.

Hall of Fame would be housed at the Naval Academy. This was clear recognition of the advances made in the reputation of sailing at the Academy. Alas, there was no appropriate place to display this magnificent collection of trophies. Nor, indeed, was there a proper administrative center for the rapidly expanding activity of sailing. The office was a drafty room in the old "Cutter Shed," not even properly heated in winter. Kauffman, Vandergrift and the Fales Committee tackled the problem, had a building designed, and went out in search of a donor. They came up with a wonderful offer from Colonel Henry Crown of Chicago whose son, Captain Robert Crown, a Reserve Officer who had fought in the Pacific and later became Chairman of the Navy League, had also died young, in 1965. The Colonel was looking for a suitable memorial, and in April of 1974 a building both impressive architecturally and functionally efficient was formally dedicated by the Colonel as The Robert Crown Sailing Center. Thus, forty years after Alf Loomis's challenging remarks, Academy sailing came of age. The Navy had come a long way from *Bullfrog* and *Alligator*.

As time went on, the solution to another problem had to be found. A number of yachts were being presented to the Academy, but in many cases the prospective donors were discouraged by the red tape that surrounded the procedure. A lengthy paper chase over an obstacle course running from the Academy on up to the desk of the Secretary of the Navy and back via a maze of "channels" had to be simplified. The solution was a suggestion by the Fales Committee for the creation of a Naval Academy Sailing Foundation. Incorporated in August of 1973, this Foundation operates exclusively for charitable purposes "to facilitate donations, to provide a source of revenue, and to acquire and hold personal property for the benefit of the sailing program of the Naval Academy." Its goal is simply to "aid, encourage and support the mission of the United States Naval Academy to enhance the education of midshipmen." The Executive Director of this organization is Colonel George W. Curran, who came to the Navy from yacht brokerage. Yachts donated to the Foundation do not have to be suitable for use at the Academy, although obviously the favorites are those with a solid racing record. The Foundation is at liberty to sell or lease the donated vessels, with the funds obtained being devoted to the mission described above.

At the time of writing, some 80 vessels, large and small, have been donated either to the Academy or to the Foundation since the days of *Vamarie*. Among them was *Jubilee III*, a 73' ketch presented by Francis Wetherill. She took over in the late 'sixties as "Queen of the Fleet" from *Freedom*. *Mareda*, a 60' yawl, and *Rage*, a 54' yawl, were both presented by Homer R. Denius in the early 'seventies. Yachts come from all sources, a famous later arrival being *Insurgence*. Her name does not appear on the donors' list, for she came via the courts, having been confiscated as a drug runner. Now affectionately known as "Pot Luck," she has been actively involved in the offshore racing program. Thus can a lady of ill repute regain her reputation in society. All of these yachts gave successful service to the midshipmen, *Jubilee III* taking a bunch of them to Spain to participate in the Race of Discovery which followed in the footsteps of Columbus, and *Rage* going south in '72 for the S.O.R.C. with two teams—a "blue" and a "gold" flown down for each event so that their studies were not interrupted. Another welcome gift was *Severn Star*, ex *Ondine*, presented by Huey Long, which together with *Maradea* made successful forays in the Bermuda races.

During the 1970s, the Navy was very much in evidence in ocean racing; but the question remained whether this level of success could be maintained. Would the swinging rhythm of success and failure continue to haunt the image of Navy sailing? Happily, in the 17 years since Jacob Vandergrift's death there has been a period of stability which gained further strength when Captain Alex Grosvenor was in command at the Navy Base. This tough and driving officer did not suffer fools gladly. He was a dedicated sailor in a hurry to get things done in a lifetime he knew would be short. On one occasion while debating a move he realized was unpopular with his Navy peers he remarked, "Well, if they want to court martial me, they will have to hurry up."

There were two things that Grosvenor recognized had to be done before anyone could relax and assume that the sailing program would remain effective. The first was to sort out the maintenance problems which would continue to exist as long as the Navy was responsible for the upkeep of yachts, and the second was that no essential continuity could be guaranteed until a permanent Director of Academy Sailing was appointed. This officer had to be a civilian, for otherwise his bi-annual rotation would recreate the very weakness under attack.

He tackled both jobs; the first by transferring a number of service billets in "Small Craft" to civilian status so that qualified shipwrights and other yacht-maintenance tradesmen could be brought in, and he captured Jack Reynolds from the Derecktor yard in Florida as overseer. Jack is still in charge of the civilian personnel in "Small Craft," but he has inherited three outstanding obstacles to efficiency which Alex Grosvenor was working to eliminate at the time of his death. (In tragic coincidence, Grosvenor, as had Jacob Vandergrift in 1969, died on the job in 1978.)

The first of these difficulties is having to adapt himself to a different boss every second or third year as a new Commander (who may never have set eyes on a yacht) is fed in to command the facility. Secondly, the service personnel who still form the nucleus of his work force are not only untrained in yacht maintenance, but often also disinterested. Even the

civilians are civil servants, which practically prohibits their being fired for laziness or incompetence without an Act of Congress. Lastly, the flow of paperwork would wash any self-respecting yard manager off his dock.

The matter of a civilian Sailing Director was brilliantly dealt with by the appointment of Graham Hall, a young man of distinction whose influence is felt to this day. This may have been the point under discussion when Grosvenor made his reference to court martial; for, while without question the job should be held by a civilian or at least a suitable retired officer, in order to get away from the inevitable rotation, the Navy has since fought to regain this position of which they were unduly jealous, and has succeeded. One thing Grosvenor did which may not have been a step in the right direction was to disband the Midshipman's Sailing Club, successor to the Midshipman's Boat Club, which had been formed in 1847 and was one of the oldest clubs to be found in the pages of the American Lloyds Register. He wanted to streamline the sailing organization and get away from charges that sailing was "fun only." He was also a strong racing enthusiast. Indeed, one of the hangovers of his reign, which was also supported by his successor, Ned Schuman (Captain E. A. Schuman III), C.O. of the Navy Base from 1978 to 1982, may have been too great an emphasis on ocean racing. There is a great difference between the tempo and specialization of training a successful racing crew and that required to shape a sound all-'round seaman. This latter function is better performed in a larger seagoing vessel with more space, a more stable platform with less gadgetry than is provided by today's racing machines. This is a subject that will require very careful judgment when the current problem of deciding upon suitable successors to the yawls is tackled. The versatility of the Luders designs will be a hard act to follow.

That said, it should be noted that Ned Schuman was responsible for a U.S. Navy triumph, a success in the face of disaster, in 1979. Having won the transatlantic race to Cork in the yacht *Alliance* against tough competition, he went on to sail the ill-fated Fastnet Race of '79, and *Alliance* came through almost unscathed to a satisfactory finish. A feather

> Annually, the sailing program covers only about 150 midshipmen. There remains a long way to go before it can be said that any significant proportion will get sail training at the Academy.

in the cap of Academy seamanship, Ned represents the third generation of a Navy family. His father, Edward Arthur Schuman, served as commanding officer of *Reina Mercedes* in the early 1950s, and remains a keen sailor still going strong as a cruisingman.

If this were to be a complete history of Academy sailing it would take more than a volume of Nautical Quarterly. The story of many yachts and yachtsmen both in and out of uniform would have to be told to illustrate the extraordinary interplay of service, civilian and social attitudes which has accompanied its development. Among those who have in recent years contributed greatly to the success of the current Academy sailing program, the names of Louise Burke and Bob Taber stand out. Louise, whose story appeared in Nautical Quarterly 6, came to the Academy at the invitation of Captain Grosvenor. Women had just started to arrive in the Academy, and he recognized the need for a woman in the sailing program. The "midshipmaids," as we used to call them in the Royal Navy, have since done very well, not only winning in intercollegiate and national dinghy events, but also proving themselves as skippers of the big boats offshore. Shortly after joining the Academy, Louise found herself sailing master of the schooner *Mistral* and was off across the Atlantic on training cruises. She now holds down a desk in the Sailing Center and continues to contribute to the excellence of the training programs. She is a sound all-'round seaman and sailor who can be relied upon to regulate the balance between racing and seamanship training already mentioned.

Bob Taber (Lieutenant General Robert C. Taber, U.S. Army retired) is a sailing soldier who has devoted his time in retirement to the promotion of a sound offshore sailing program for the midshipmen. He has captained no fewer than five transatlantic cruises—first in *Mistral*, lately in *Astral*, the current queen of the Academy fleet, a 92' motorsailer donated in 1979 by Cornelius C. Vanderstar. These cruises were begun with the enthusiastic support of Admiral William McKee, then Superintendent, who started the scheme of giving the midshipmen cruise credits for offshore sailing voyages during their summer sea-duty training periods.

When Graham Hall resigned in 1981 to become Vice President of Horizon Sails in Norwalk, Patrick Healy, later to be stolen by the Canadians to coach their Olympic team, became Intercollegiate Director, and continued the good work. His place was in turn taken by Mike Waters, himself a graduate of the Academy. That Mike has sustained the record of his predecessors is indicated by the fact that the Leonard M. Fowle Trophy, awarded annually in intercollegiate yacht racing for the best overall performance in the five ACYRA championships (Dinghy, Team Racing, Women's, Singlehanded and Sloop), has been won by the Academy continuously for the last five years. Undoubtedly this successful record has been greatly abetted by fellow dinghy coach Susan Dierdorff,

herself a woman's world singlehanded championship contender. While this is an enviable record, it is also one that must be put into the perspective of a student body numbering some four thousand. Annually, the sailing program, with the exception of a short familiarization session in the knockabouts for the plebes, covers only about 150 midshipmen. There remains a long way to go before it can be said that any significant proportion, even of the seagoing executive officers, will get sail training at the Academy.

There are, however, reasons for optimism. One important step taken by the Navy is that, as of last year, sailing qualifications earned by midshipmen at the Academy will be fed into their computer records at the Bureau of Personnel. This will go a long way to prevent the adverse effects of what one might call "the billet mentality." This essentially dictates that, because all naval officers are so highly trained, it is only necessary to feed an individual of suitable rank into a particular slot, and he or she will be able to fulfill its "job description." Recently, for instance, young lieutenants and ensigns have been appointed back from the fleet to teach midshipmen seamanship and sail training. It was accepted that they themselves would first have to learn to sail, a process that was to be completed in terms of weeks. The idea that instant sailing instructors can be produced almost overnight is remarkable. An intriguing example of this philosophy was the discovery by the officer in charge of navigation training that the appointee required to teach sextant navigation to the mids was a pregnant lady who had not been to sea.

This article touches only some of the highlights in this century of the uphill struggle to establish and maintain adequate sail-training facilities at the Naval Academy. It also illustrates the outstanding contribution which has been made to this program by yachtsmen outside the service. As yachting has become increasingly popular as a participant sport, so the image of a young naval officer at a loss in a small boat becomes more incongruous. There is no denying the importance of a high standard of education required by the modern naval officer; however, a suitably prepared "athletic bookworm" does not seem to be all the answer. He or she must also possess the ability to set an example, to oversee and assist the variety of technical specialists who will be under command, a very considerable number of whom will still be seamen. There is no better training for the art of seamanship than the small sailing vessel at sea. While it will be the ambition of every red-blooded midship-man or -maid to become involved in intercollegiate sailing competition and advance to "national" or "Olympic" stature, the emphasis of sail training at the Academy should focus on giving as many as possible a good grounding in small-boat handling. And it should encourage the simple enjoyment of being on the water. Participation in racing programs should then be the reward for those showing the greatest aptitude in this professional training.

In the Fleets and Shore Establishments, the Directorate of Sail Training has made exciting progress in the encouragement of interest in sailing. Yachts are also being introduced to the R.O.T.C. programs, and this is improving their popularity and the standard both of applicants and participants.

At the Academy, the current fleet consists of about a dozen Class A donated yachts, the ocean training ship *Astral*, 12 fiberglass yawls, 6 Shields sloops, 30 420 dinghies, 24 Lasers, 30 Rainbow knockabouts, and a "shoal" of sailboards recently presented. These last, needless to say, are very popular with the midshipmen. This may seem a very adequate fleet until one remembers that it has to serve 4000 candidates for instruction, plus all the intercollegiate events and the annual summer offshore cruises now undertaken, in addition to participation in many ocean-racing events. This summer, some 160 midshipmen will be involved in offshore cruises in nine or ten of the celebrated yawls and in three IOR yachts. These cruises will take the yawls to Bermuda and to Beaufort, North Carolina. *Enterprise* and *Insurgent* will sail south to Bermuda, take part in the Tall Ships Race from Bermuda to Halifax, then join the parade of Tall Ships and small ships up the St. Lawrence to Quebec. The youngsters fortunate enough to put this experience under their belts will, in seagoing experience, steal a good march upon their contemporaries who will have spent their summer in the "grey funnels."

The current state of cooperation between the Naval Authorities and the Fales Committee is excellent. The Sailing Foundation is doing a sterling job of encouraging donations, but the permanent staff of instructors remains pitifully small. Problems also remain in the administrative and maintenance procedures. In both areas there still exists a need for the vital skilled continuity which the Navy cannot provide without a flexibility in the system which would permit them to leave the right men in the right job just so long as their skills remain adequate. It takes a good two years for the right man to pick up all the threads of the various institutions and tasks involved, let alone start knitting a good pattern. In the opinion of the author, until the Fleets are in a position to feed back suitably highly skilled and experienced sailors capable of operating a sail-training program at "national" level, which is still a few years into the future, a Civilian Director of Sailing should be appointed with a salary similar to that of the football coach! Alongside him, the Civilian Yard Manager with a suitably trained permanent staff should be responsible for all maintenance. These two, working effectively together in the excellent facilities which now exist, would soon remove the incompatibility between efficient yacht operation and the inflexibility and constant mobility of naval customs and procedures which are neither designed for nor suited to this purpose.

Finally, if any larger training yachts are to be operated offshore, the *Vamarie* lesson must be learned once and for all time. A permanent professional crew of considerable skill and experience must be allocated to such a vessel in the interests of maintenance standards, operational procedures and, above all these days, safety!

One trusts that these problems will be solved, as those of the past have been—not easily, of course, but inevitably. And, to answer Alf Loomis's question: yes, there are some sailors in the Navy—better ones all the time.

At right, the yawls in a training exercise on their home waters in Annapolis. In addition to sail-training and intercollegiate competition on the Chesapeake, the yawls range farther afield, especially during the summer offshore cruises. Some 160 midshipmen will be sailing nine or ten of them, along with a few IOR yachts, in offshore cruises to Bermuda and to Beaufort, North Carolina, this summer. The yawls *Enterprise* and *Insurgent* are joining the Tall Ships fleet at Bermuda for the race to Halifax and the parade of vessels up the St. Lawrence to Quebec, celebrating the 450th anniversary of Jacques Cartier's voyage to French Canada.

NAUTICAL QUARTERLY

When I had written my books on whales and on porpoises and dolphins, I was asked to do the same for the rest of the aquatically-oriented, warm-blooded creatures; to describe and illustrate the seals, sea lions, walruses, manatees, et al. At first I thought it would be easy: I would just tackle the task as I had with the cetaceans; do the research, paint the pictures, and *voilà*, a third tome. □ It was not that easy. I painted the "field guide" illustrations of all these left-over marine mammals, but then I became discouraged. They all seemed so much alike. Oh, there were differences, of course; the sea lions had visible ears, while those of the seals were only pinholes; the sea lions could move their hind flippers, and therefore walk (more or less) adequately on land, while the seals, who could not rotate their hind flippers forward, had to hunch along like giant inchworms. They had a variety of color patterns: there were ribbon seals and ringed seals, and others that had a "harp" pattern or the spots of a leopard. The walruses have those incredible tusks, and there is a species of seal known as the crabeater, which does not eat crabs at all, but feeds on the shrimp-like crustaceans known as krill, the food of the baleen whales. Then there were the sirenians: manatees and dugongs, which are ungainly, ugly animals (although there are stories that early seafarers confused them with mermaids). There were even some other creatures, such as the polar bear and the sea otter, which may not be accurately classified as marine mammals at all, since they can (and do) spend most of their time on land.

A DIVERSITY OF SEALS

BY RICHARD ELLIS

I was faced with this grab bag of miscellaneous mammals, of which some had flippers, some had legs, some spent all their lives in the water, and others spent a lot of time on terra firma. How was I going to incorporate this diversity into a coherent book? It seemed to me that the pinnipeds (the seals and sea lions), sirenians (manatees, dugongs and the extinct Steller's Sea Cow), and the bears and otters were better characterized by their differences than by their similarities. Paradoxically, it also seemed that the seals and sea lions were too much alike: they all swam around for a while, then hauled out on a beach or on the ice, fought each other noisily, and then mated, ready to begin the cycle again. Whereas the first two books had almost named themselves—*The Book of Whales*, and *Dolphins and Porpoises*—I couldn't even think of a name for this one. "Seals, Sea Lions, Walruses, Manatees, Dugongs, Polar Bears and Sea Otters?" Too long. "Miscellaneous Marine Mammals?" Too weak. "Fur and Flippers?" Too silly.

But because I am nothing if not a creature of habit (and one who honors contracts), I began the research. Much to my surprise and pleasure, I discovered that I was wrong in almost all my preconceptions. Rather than being boringly similar, the pinnipeds are extraordinarily diverse. And of course the manatees are sui generis, aquatic mammals that are unlike any other creatures on earth. To point up this uniqueness, let us begin with the fabulous sea cow, which no longer exists.

In 1741, the Danish explorer Vitus Bering was shipwrecked on the Commander Islands off the coast of Siberia, one of which now bears his name, as does the sea north of the Aleutian Islands. On these islands, Bering and his crew encountered some very unusual animals; they were apparently the first Europeans to see the northern fur seal, the northern sea lion, the sea otter, and the blue fox. Bering had been charged by his employer Czar Peter to "discover everything that has not been discovered," and despite the ill-fated voyage of his ship *St. Peter*, he seemed on the way to doing just that. In addition to the seals and sea lions, Bering discovered one of the most unusual animals on earth, an animal that, unfortunately, survived its "discovery" by only 27 years.

Because it was an enormous, slow-moving creature that wallowed and grazed in the inshore waters, it was a godsend to the stranded seamen. The animals were easily killed, and provided great quantities of meat and oil for the Russian crew and officers. Its thick skin was used for bootsoles and also for the manufacture of skin boats, known as *baidars*. Also aboard Bering's ship was the German naturalist Georg Wilhelm Steller. Following Steller's published descriptions of the newly discovered animals, his name has been permanently associated with them.

It looked very much like today's manatee or dugong (but there is no reason to assume that Bering, Steller, or anyone else on the voyage had ever seen a manatee or a dugong, or even knew of their existence). It had a fat, ungainly body; short, flipper-like forelimbs, and a horizontal tail, like that of a whale. This animal, which would eventually acquire the name *Hydrodamalis gigas* ("giant sea cow"), differed dramatically from its relatives, because it was immense. While the other sirenians rarely reach a length of twelve feet, the sea cow measured more than thirty feet. Although they were never weighed (how could they be?), modern researchers have estimated their weight at upwards of eight tons. According to Steller's description, the sea cow had the foreparts of a seal, and the hind end of a fish. It had a skull "like that of a horse." Instead of teeth, it had flattened, ridged plates in the upper and lower jaws, which it used to masticate the seaweed on which it fed. Its skin was dark brown, becoming blackish when wet, and heavily wrinkled and scored, "like the bark of a tree." A piece of this inch-thick skin is on exhibit today in the museum in Leningrad.

One scientist has suggested that the four-inch coating of blubber beneath the skin made the animal so buoyant that it could not totally submerge, and therefore it had to feed in water shallow enough to allow it to reach the bottom without diving. This propensity to remain in shallow water made sea cows ridiculously easy to kill; all the hunters had to do was wade into the waist-deep water and spear them. There was, however, the problem of hauling the five- to eight- ton animals ashore for butchering. Sea cows often had white spots on their skin—perhaps healed scars—and the tail was two-lobed like that of a dolphin, but noticeably tattered on the trailing edge.

The forelimbs of the manatee and the dugong contain the normal mammalian "manus," or hand bones. But Steller's sea cow differed from its smaller relatives—and from every other mammal as well—in that it had no phalanges or finger bones in its forelimbs. Its arms stopped at the "elbow," and they have been described (in a 1922 translation from the 1742 Russian description), as "having the appearance of being amputated and...covered with coarse, calloused skin and shaped much like a horse's hoof, doubled over in a hook." *Hydrodamalis* evidently used these strange appendages to pull itself along the shallow bottom, or perhaps to scoop seaweed and algae into its mouth.

The sea cow is now extinct, and it has been since a Russian sealer killed the last one in 1768. It took only 27 years for man to discover the giant sea cow, then eliminate it from the face of the earth. One cannot hold Bering, Steller, or the sealers completely responsible for this unprecedented act; they could hardly have known that the population they discovered on these remote islands represented the last of the sea cows. For all they knew, there would be many more islands to discover, and probably many more strange new creatures, including more of the immense sea cows.

Now the other, smaller sirenians are in trouble. All three species of manatees—the Florida and West Indian, the Amazonian, and the West African—are hunted for their blubber and meat, except in Florida, where they are protected from hunters but not from the propellers of powerboats. It seems that these placid, slow-moving creatures cannot avoid the fast-moving boats, and they are frequently run over and severely injured—often killed.

The dugong, which bears a strong resemblance to its cousin, differs in the shape of its tail: Where the manatee has a rounded, paddle-like appendage, the dugong's tail has twin flukes, like that of a whale or dolphin. While little is known of the distribution of this animal, it has been reported throughout the Indo-Pacific region, from East Africa to Southeast Asia, and south to northern Australia. In almost all of its range, the dugong is hunted for food and, in at least one area, it is further threatened by technology (and politics) gone wild. In the Persian Gulf, where an enormous oil fire has been burning for years, the dugongs are being burned to death. The ongoing war between Iran and Iraq has made extinguishing this fire impossible. In addition to the prodigality of thousands of gallons of oil going up in smoke every day, and the resultant pollution, the hapless dugong suffers mightily.

And now to the pinnipeds—the seals and sea lions. Rather than being monotonously similar, the pinnipeds are fascinating in their diversity. Yes, they all come ashore to breed and deliver their young, and yes, they all have fur coats and

> The sea cow is now extinct, and it has been since a Russian sealer killed the last one in 1768. It took only 27 years for man to discover the giant sea cow, then eliminate it from the face of the earth.

whiskers, technically known as *vibrissae*. But within the order Pinnepedia—the name means "feather-" or "fin-foot"—there is a remarkable variety of size, shape, habit and habitat.

The largest of the pinnipeds is the elephant seal, named not so much for its size—although it is huge—but for the elongated proboscis of the 20-foot, four-ton males. These abbreviated trunks contribute substantially to the unattractiveness of an already ugly animal. The snout develops only in the adult bulls, and the babies and females are not nearly as ugly, with their short noses and dark, liquid eyes. As with most pinnipeds, the bulls are larger than the females, a development that is useful in the battles for females and territorial dominance.

The gigantic elephant seals are among the most notorious fighters of all the pinnipeds. After they arrive on the breeding beaches, the bulls stake out their territories and defend them energetically against interlopers. The ensuing battles rarely end in death, but serious injuries occasionally result from the slashing canine teeth, powered by the heavily muscled head and neck. (One of the problems with having a long nose is that it often gets in the way, and is frequently bitten). The dominant males mate with their assembled harems, and in the following year—usually on the same beach—their young are born. After about four weeks, the pups are abandoned by their mothers and must fend for themselves.

Elephant seals feed on various kinds of fish, and they are believed to be excellent divers. No one knows much about these animals when they are away from the beaches, since they seem to disappear. In other words, we do not really know where they go when they are not hauled out and visible on the rocky shores of the California islands (and now the mainland; one bull came ashore at Pebble Beach during a golf tournament some years ago) and on various island groups in the high latitudes of the Southern Hemisphere—the Crozets, South Shetlands, Falklands, South Georgia, and the Valdés Peninsula in southern Argentina. Both the northern and southern species of elephant seals were severely depleted by sealers in the nineteenth century who hunted them for their plentiful oil and blubber. But under the protection of various governments, both populations have revived. In fact, the California population is almost too numerous. From a low of perhaps fifty animals in 1892, there are now 60,000+ elephant seals. They have begun to colonize many new areas, including Año Nuevo on the mainland, across the channel from Año Nuevo

Various species of seals and sea lions are shown on these pages. Here, hauled out on an icy shelf of Paradise Bay, two crabeater seals look content in their frozen habitat. Although crabeater seals have been unmolested by man, there is fear that one of the seal-hunting nations will attempt to harvest this plentiful species. On pages 84 & 85, a bull and his females pose for the camera on their South Georgia Island home. These regal-looking creatures are Kerguelan Fur Seals, one of the eight species of the genus *Arctocephalus*, meaning "bearheaded," a reference to the male's shaggy head and neck ruff. In the photo on page 82, it's hard to tell where the Steller's Sea Lions end and the rocks of Round Island, Alaska, begin. They are extremely wary of people and difficult to approach on land. On page 88, a pair of California sea lions bask in the sun.

Island. There is probably not enough room on the California mainland for breeding colonies of bawling, grunting, fighting elephant seals—which may be dangerous to humans during the time the two are in the same place—so a new problem has arisen: what do you do about too many of these creatures?

The walrus is the next largest of the pinnipeds, but it is not exactly a seal, nor is it a sea lion. It is an animal unto itself, with some of the characteristics of seals, some of sea lions, and some that make it unique among the pinnipeds. The great ivory tusks, which may reach a length of three feet in adult males, are among the most curious structures in the animal kingdom. At first, it was assumed that the walrus used them for feeding (both males and females have tusks), to dig up the clams that make up their diet. But when the soft parts of the clams and not the shells were found in the walrus' stomachs, this theory had to be discarded. Although no one has actually seen a walrus feed in the wild, it is now assumed that they plow along the bottom using their tusks like sled runners, locate the buried clams by means of their sensitive, bewhiskered muzzles, and then suck the clams from their shells. But, if the tusks are not used for feeding, then what purpose do these shafts of ivory serve? Biologists believe that they are used to demonstrate dominance; the biggest and most powerful bulls have the largest tusks, and therefore they attract the receptive females. (While it is not known for certain how the walrus uses his or her tusks, it is very clear for what purpose the Eskimos use these elongated teeth. Thousands of walrus are killed every year for the tusks to be carved into ivory artifacts for sale, and the carcasses are left to rot on the beaches).

The smaller pinnipeds are just as interesting as their gigantic cousins. The earless seals, known collectively as Phocidae, from the Greek *phoca*, which simply means "seal," are found throughout the temperate and polar waters of the world, always close to the land or the pack ice. Only the tropical monk seals inhabit warmer waters, and these may represent only relict populations, on their way to extinction. In fact, the Caribbean monk seal, one of the three species of monk seals (genus *Monachus*), is already extinct, having been last reported from Jamaica in 1952. There are probably no more than 100 Mediterranean monk seals on the islands off North Africa. The only species of warm-water seal that exists in any significant numbers is the Hawaiian variety, found mostly in the Leeward Islands of the Hawaiian chain. There are only about 700 of these rare creatures left. But because of the remoteness of their habitat—very few tourists visit French Frigate

Shoals, Pearl & Hermes Islands or Laysan—there is hope for their survival. No one, however, has told the tiger sharks about this endangered species; they prey on the slow-swimming monk seals regularly, representing the only threat to these isolated animals.

Probably the best known of the earless seals is the harbor seal, which is distributed throughout the temperate and arctic waters of the Northern Hemisphere. The little spotted seal can often be seen hauled out on sandy or rocky beaches from Greenland to Maine on the east coast of North America, and from Alaska to California on the west. It can also be found in England and Scotland, and from the Bering Sea to Japan. These little seals frequently raid fishermen's nets, and there are many areas where they are shot on sight. Still, recent estimates indicate that there are perhaps a million harbor seals left throughout their extensive range. They are also among the most common marine mammals in captivity, since they have no compunctions about breeding in zoos and aquariums. Because of this propensity, there have been no collections of wild specimens for exhibit for many years: all the harbor seals in captivity are either rehabilitated stranders or captive-born animals.

Follow the line of 60° north latitude around the globe, and you will pretty much define the range of the northern "ice seals." (A corresponding situation exists in the Southern Hemisphere, south of the Antarctic Convergence, or about 50° south.) From Siberia to Greenland, from Hudson Bay to Alaska, there can be found a variety of earless seals (and an occasional otariid as well), that use the ice or the rocky island beaches as "haul-out" or breeding areas. In the north, we find the ringed, bearded, ribbon, harp, and Baikal seals, as well as the ubiquitous harbor seal.

Ringed seals, named for the pattern of grayish rings on a darker ground, are the only seals that are born in caves or tunnels in the snow. These lairs are dug by the gravid females as they prepare to give birth, and the pups spend the first couple of months of their lives in the (comparatively) warm surroundings of this ice tunnel. Polar bears prey on these small (maximum length: 4½ feet) seals by waiting for them to appear at their breathing holes in the ice, then swiping them from the water with their massive, lethally-clawed front paws.

Another uniquely colored seal is the ribbon seal. Born white, these seals begin to develop a series of broad, cream-colored ribbons on a coat of chocolate brown. Like its close relative the ringed seal (both are members of the genus *Phoca*, as are the harp and harbor seals), this is not an endangered species. There are not enough polar bears—which, interestingly, are considered endangered—or Eskimos to threaten the populations of these Arctic seals, and estimates of some populations run as high as 100,000 in a given area.

The harp seal, *Phoca groenlandica*, has been the object of an intensive "harvest," and more importantly, the focus of a highly-publicized conservation effort. The battle has been confined to Newfoundland, although the species is found from Hudson Bay to Greenland (hence its scientific name), and from northern Norway to northern Russia. The harp seal, whose common name is derived from the vaguely "harplike" pattern on the adults, is born white, fluffy, and cuter than almost any baby animal has a right to be. It is the clubbing of these "whitecoats" by the Newfoundlanders in their annual seal hunt that has generated all the adverse attention.

"Save the Seals" posters and bumper stickers, all showing a sloe-eyed, helpless, adorable baby seal, have galvanized a massive protest movement, accompanied by acts of violence, fistfights, dyeing baby seals green, government action, and finally, the shutting down of the seal hunt. Seal skins may no longer be exported from Canada to the European Economic Community (EEC) countries. Since 1972, the United States has had the marine Mammal Protection Act in place, banning the import of any marine mammal products.

Before we wrench our arms out of their sockets patting ourselves on the back, however, we should consider the other great seal kill in North American waters: the hunt of the northern fur seal in the Pribilof Islands. *Callorhinus ursinus* (whose name can be roughly translated as "pretty-faced sea bear"), was hunted indiscriminately by Russian, Japanese, Canadian and American sealers until the treaty of 1917 set limits on the numbers that could be killed. Since 1976, the only people allowed to kill the fur seals are the Pribilof Islanders, and they kill some 25,000 annually. They do it by clubbing the young males, the same way that the Newfoundlanders killed the whitecoats, and they do it with the cognizance and cooperation of the United States government. Since the skins cannot be imported into the U.S., they are either shipped to Russia or Japan, or stored—along with the carcasses—in the Pribilofs.

If the seals of the Northern Hemisphere have been traditionally harassed by sealers, Eskimos and polar bears (and killer whales, the ocean's dominant predator of warm-blooded prey), those of the Southern regions have been virtually ignored. Of the potential predators, only the killer whale inhabits the southern oceans; there

The harp seal is born white, fluffy, and cuter than almost any baby animal has a right to be. It is the clubbing of these "whitecoats" by the Newfoundlanders that has generated so much adverse attention.

are no Eskimos, polar bears or sealers in the Antarctic. The seals exist in almost uncountable numbers in the most inaccessible part of the globe: it might be said that the Antarctic belongs to the seals. There are several varieties of phocids here of which little is known because of the remoteness of their habitat. The Ross seal, named for the Antarctic explorer James Clark Ross (1800-1862) is one of these. It is the smallest of the Antarctic seals, rarely reaching a length of seven feet. We know hardly anything about its natural history, but it emits sounds that have been variously described as "gurgling," "clucking," "sniffling," and "snorting." Also found in these trackless, icy wastes is the Weddell seal. This creature of the cold is named for another Antarctic explorer, James Weddell (1787-1834), for whom also the Weddell Sea is named. *Leptonychotes weddelli* is, in all likelihood, the deep-diving champion of the phocid world. These big-bodied, small-headed seals can dive to depths of 2000 feet or more, and stay submerged for an hour.

The leopard seal is at the opposite end of the physical spectrum. In contrast to the Weddells, whose head seems much too small for its fat body, the head of the leopard seal appears to be much too large. The leopard seal is named not so much for its spots, but for its temperament. While most other seals feed on fish, crustaceans or squid, *Hydrurga* prefers penguins. After catching its flightless prey, the leopard seal holds the penguin in its massive jaws and, armed with powerful canine teeth (another similarity to its terrestrial namesake), literally shakes the bird out of its skin before devouring it.

The crabeater seal (*Lobodon carcinophagus*) does not eat crabs at all, but eats krill, the food of the baleen whales. It has specially designed, multi-cusped teeth, which are believed to function like a sieve, straining the shrimp-like crustaceans from the water. Although accurate census figures are not available, the crabeater is extremely abundant. Estimates of the total population run as high as 75 million animals. Even if these figures are exaggerated, there is no question that the crabeater seal is one of the most numerous large mammals in the world.

From deep in the Southern Hemisphere all the way to the Pribilofs, wherever there are beaches for sea lions to haul out on, there are eared seals to haul out on them. Sea lions and fur seals are similar animals, with dense, thick fur and visible ears. In all cases, the males are larger than the females, and in some species, such as Steller's sea lion, the bulls are three times as large as the cows. The best known of all the sea lions, of course, is the California sea lion, *Zalophus californianus*. This is the "trained seal"—although it is not a seal at all, but a proper sea lion—of zoos and circuses, often seen clapping its flippers and balancing objects on its nose. It is found from British Columbia south to Baja California with a subspecific population in the Galapagos Islands. As with all sea lions, the bulls are considerably larger than the cows, and the mature males develop a pronounced "forehead" as they reach the breeding age. Like the harbor seals, California sea lions are often stranded and collected for zoos and aquariums, and there have been several generations born in captivity.

Because of their luxurious coats, the fur seals were the primary objects of the sealers of the 18th and 19th centuries, but they were reported as early as Magellan's 1520 voyage around Cape Horn. There are sea lion species in New Zealand, Australia, South America, and the North Pacific. Fur seals (genus *Arctocephalus*) live throughout the Southern Ocean, in a circumantarctic distribution that incorporates southern South America, South Africa, New Zealand, Australia, and various island groups. Fur seals are also found in the Galapagos and the islands off the coast of Baja California. Most of them are similar in morphology and coloration, with pointed snouts and grizzled, gray-brown pelage. Most of the species were intensively hunted by sealers, and the current status of the various populations is a function of the intensity of these hunts. The precipitous decrease in their populations seems to have been arrested since all species of southern fur seals are now protected by national legislation.

As I learned more about the seals and sea lions, I realized that they were anything but the one-note animals that I thought they were. Instead of a bunch of sausage-shaped critters that barked, fought and swam around, they are as varied and interesting as any group of animals that I have ever studied. From pole to pole—and in virtually all the waters in between—they present an aspect of natural history that is so varied and diverse that they cannot be covered in a short piece like this one. Rather, a whole book is called for, and even this will only skim the surface. Now inspired by my preliminary research, I am off to the library (and perhaps California, Alaska, or the Antarctic), to *really* go to work. I have already dived with the southern sea lions of Valdés Peninsula, Argentina, and been chased from the water by an angry, growling bull, but that is another story. What I need now is a title. How about "The Fascinating World of the Pinnipeds?" "The Divers?" "Mammals of Land and Water?" Any suggestions will be welcome.

After catching its flightless prey, the leopard seal holds the penguin in its massive jaws and, armed with powerful canine teeth, literally shakes the bird out of its skin before devouring it.

A GUIDE TO THE IDENTIFICATION OF SEALS & SEA LIONS

STELLER'S SEA LION
(EUMETOPIAS JUBATUS)

Distribution: The North Pacific only. Breeds in the Pribilofs, Aleutians, and the North American coast to southern California.

This is the largest of all eared seals: adult males weigh up to one ton; females up to 700 pounds. They are wary of humans. There are approximately 300,000 in the world today.

CALIFORNIA SEA LION
(ZALOPHUS CALIFORNIANUS)

Distribution: California waters, with subspecies in Galapagos and Japan.

They are often erroneously called "trained seals" in circuses, but are true sea lions. Males are much larger and heavier than females, reaching 600 pounds, and developing a prominent "sagittal crest" or forehead.

AUSTRALIAN SEA LION
(NEOPHOCA CINEREA)

Distribution: The coasts of southern Australia only. They are one of the few species that is non-migratory.

These animals were severely decimated by sealers in the 18th and 19th centuries. It is estimated that there are no more than 5000 left today. They are renowned for their ability to move about on land.

NEW ZEALAND SEA LION
(PHOCARCTOS HOOKERI)

Distribution: Found mostly in the subantarctic islands of New Zealand. Sometimes seen on South Island.

This species is also known as Hooker's sea lion. As with all sea lions, the males grow much larger, and may reach 10 feet in length and weigh 800 pounds. Dominant males collect "harems" and defend them against intruding bulls.

SOUTHERN SEA LION
(OTARIA FLAVESCENS)

Distribution: Both coasts of southern South America, from Peru to Cape Horn on the west, and north to Uruguay on the east coast.

Males have a "mane" that gives them their common name. Females are smaller and lighter in color. Primarily a fish-eater, this seal is often seen in shallow inshore waters. There are about 275,000 living on both coasts.

SOUTHERN FUR SEAL
(ARCTOCEPHALUS spp.)

Distribution: There are eight species in this genus, all but one found south of the Equator. They are distinguished primarily by geography, and inhabit the Southern Hemisphere island groups such as the Kerguelens, the Falklands, Juan Fernandez, and also South Australia, South Africa, and both coasts of southern South America. The smallest in size, the Guadalupe, is found off the coast of Baja California.

NORTHERN FUR SEAL
(CALLORHINUS URSINUS)

Distribution: Breeds on the chain of islands from Alaska to Kamchatka, Siberia. Found as far south as Santa Barbara, California, in the eastern North Pacific, and Honshu, Japan, in the west.

Once hunted mercilessly, they are now "harvested" only in the Pribilofs, and under an agreement between the U.S., Japan, Canada, and the USSR, some 25,000 are killed annually for their fur.

WALRUS
(ODOBENUS ROSMARUS)

Distribution: There are two subspecies, the Pacific and the Atlantic. Both inhabit the rocky islands of the Arctic.

Males are larger than females. Both sexes have tusks. They have never been observed feeding in the wild. They are hunted by Eskimos for food and ivory, and their numbers are declining throughout their range.

HARBOR SEAL
(PHOCA VITULINA)

Distribution: Found throughout the Northern Hemisphere, it has the widest distribution of any pinniped.

A non-migratory species, they breed and feed in the same area. They eat almost anything they catch, but their diet consists mostly of fish. They occasionally raid fishermen's nets and are killed for this reason, as well as for their meat and fur.

RINGED SEAL
(PUSA HISPIDA)

Distribution: The Northern Hemisphere ice pack

The smallest of the earless seals, ringed seals rarely reach 4½ feet in length. Females give birth in caves or tunnels in the snow. Eskimos hunt them for their meat, blubber and skins, and polar bears prey on them. There are several subspecies, primarily distinguished by distribution.

BAIKAL SEAL
(PUSA SIBIRICA)

Distribution: Lake Baikal in Siberia

The only completely freshwater seal, this species is similar in size and shape to the ringed seal, but its coat is usually brown or yellowish without rings or spots. Little is known of this species, except that they are hunted in large numbers by the Siberians.

RIBBON SEAL
(HISTRIOPHOCA FASCIATA)

Distribution: Found only in the Arctic North Pacific, from Alaska to northern Japan.

They are born white, but after several weeks they shed and acquire the broad "ribbons" that characterize the adult pelage. They are indifferent to the approach of predators: polar bears, arctic foxes, or humans. They are hunted by Siberian sealers and Eskimos.

HARP SEAL
(PAGOPHILUS GROENLANDICUS)

Distribution: Found throughout the Northern Hemisphere ice pack from Canada to Greenland and Siberia.

They are born white, but within a month they begin to develop the coloration of adults. The "whitecoats" (pups) are clubbed to death by the Newfoundland sealers. These seals are extremely aquatic, and spend much of their lives in the water.

GREY SEAL
(HALICHOERUS GRYPUS)

Distribution: Largest concentration around the British Isles, although they are found in Canada and in northwestern Europe.

They are sometimes confused with harbor seals. Greys are larger, with a longer snout, accounting for the Canadian name "horse-head." They are the subject of controversy between the fishermen who kill them and the conservationists who would protect them.

BEARDED SEAL
(ERIGNATHUS BARBATUS)

Distribution: Northern Hemisphere

Their long whiskers ("vibrissae") are responsible for their name. Males grow larger than females, and can reach 12 feet. Bearded seals are very vocal, and they are among the few mammals that "sing." They are hunted for their meat, blubber and skins.

MEDITERRANEAN MONK SEAL
(MONACHUS MONACHUS)

Distribution: The Mediterranean, North Africa, Madeira

There are probably no more than 1000 of these seals left since their habitat is being increasingly invaded by humans. They never have developed the ability to escape on land, and people are able to walk right up to them. Considered endangered, there are fears that this species will not survive the 20th century.

CARIBBEAN MONK SEAL
(MONACHUS TROPICALIS)

First described by Columbus in 1494, this seal had been seen around various Caribbean islands such as the Antilles, the Bahamas, and even the Florida Keys. Since the last documented sighting took place in 1952 off Jamaica, this species is now thought to be totally extinct, the result of its having been displaced and hunted by men since the discovery of these islands.

HAWAIIAN MONK SEAL
(MONACHUS SCHAUINSLANDI)

Distribution: Found primarily in the Leeward Islands, they occasionally stray to the main Hawaiian group.

They were undisturbed until WWII when U.S. forces occupied Laysan and Midway. As of 1978, there were fewer than 700 of them. They are fully protected now, but are particularly susceptible to predation by tiger sharks.

CRABEATER SEAL
(LOBODON CARCINOPHAGUS)

Distribution: The Antarctic

The crabeater seal is the most numerous of all pinnipeds, with estimates of its population ranging from 15-75 million. It is one of the most abundant large mammals in the world. Contrary to its name, it feeds primarily on "krill," the small euphausiid shrimp that is also eaten by the baleen whales.

WEDDELL SEAL
(LEPTONYCHOTES WEDDELLI)

Distribution: Antarctic

These seals were named for the Antarctic explorer James Weddell. They spend a great deal of time under the ice, breaking holes in the ice with specially developed canine teeth. They are among the most accomplished divers of all pinnipeds; they can remain submerged for over an hour and descend to almost 2000 feet.

LEOPARD SEAL
(HYDRURGA LEPTONYX)

Distribution: Throughout the Antarctic and surrounding island groups.

Named for its spots as well as its predaceous habits, the leopard seal is an active carnivore, feeding on fish, krill, squid, other seals, and penguins. This species is unusual in that the females are considerably larger than the males. Both sexes have a large head.

HOODED SEAL
(CYSTOPHORA CRISTATA)

Distribution: The arctic and subarctic North Atlantic off Labrador, Greenland, and Jan Mayen Land.

They get their name from the inflatable nasal sac that occurs only in mature males, and is believed to be part of the dominance hierarchy, used to intimidate subordinate males. Excellent divers, a month-old pup made a record dive of 250 feet.

SOUTHERN ELEPHANT SEAL
(MIROUNGA LEONINA)

Distribution: Found throughout island groups in the Southern Ocean, including South Georgia, Macquarie, Kerguelen, Heard, Marion, and the Falklands. Also at Valdés Peninsula on the Patagonian coast of Argentina.

At a length of 20 feet, the bulls of this species are the largest of all the pinnipeds. Females only grow to 12 feet.

DUGONG
(DUGONG DUGON)

Distribution: A widely distributed but uncommon animal of the east African and Indo-Pacific coasts.

Dugongs are vegetarians, grazing cowlike on the bottom, and then surfacing slowly to breathe. They spend their entire lives in water. Dugongs are hunted so heavily for their meat, oil and blubber that, although there are few accurate estimates of their population, they are considered endangered.

CARIBBEAN MANATEE
(TRICHECHUS MANATUS)

Distribution: Found in the coastal waters of the southeastern U.S., through the Caribbean, to the northern coast of South America.

This is a fat, fully aquatic mammal, reaching a length of 10 feet and a weight of over 500 pounds. They feed on water plants, and are so efficient at it that they are used to clear clogged waterways of plants. In Florida, these lethargic animals are endangered by fast-moving motorboats that run over them.

STELLER'S SEA COW
(HYDRODAMALIS GIGAS)

This huge sirenian was discovered by Georg Steller, the naturalist aboard Captain Vitus Bering's expedition to the North Pacific in 1742. By 1769, it was extinct, killed off for food and leather by the Russian sealers that were stopping off at the Commander Islands. It probably reached a length of 30 feet, and may have weighed as much as four tons. It fed on seaweed, and there is speculation that it was too buoyant to dive.

CENTURION 47
A SURVEY BY FRASER FRASER-HARRIS

Henri Wauquiez, fiftyish, is a big man who moves fast and is full of enthusiasm. His father, who owned the tannery in which Henri began his business career, collected and restored old racing cars, and his favorites were Bugattis. Appreciation of quality and performance is obviously a family tradition.

The story of Henri's entry into the yachting world is a delightful example of lively ambition grasping opportunity, even in adversity. In 1964 he bought an Elizabethan 29, a performance cruising boat built by the English designer Peter Webster. Shortly after its commissioning in St. Tropez, an admirer on the dock said it was the sort of boat he wanted, and asked who was the French agent? Knowing it to be the only Elizabethan 29 in France, and always the salesman, Henri said that he was. The man replied that he would buy one provided it could be delivered the following spring. Henri contacted Peter Webster only to be told that the order book was already overflowing. There remained a solution. If Webster would lend him the molds, and his father would lease him some space in the tannery at Mouvaux, he could build the boat himself. Despite the fact that Henri had never built a boat in his life, that is exactly what was done. Peter Webster brought over the molds, supervised the construction, and introduced Henri to the art of building a good boat. At the same time, the tanning business was on the way down. Throughout the world, rubber and plastic were replacing shoe leather. Tanneries were hard hit, and Wauquiez of Mouvaux was the biggest in France. Thus the great tanning vats were emptied and became production bays; the 1901 crane that had moved loads of hides was put to work moving boats.

Henri's father retired from the tannery, moved down to Port Grimaud to run the agency there and sell boats. He only retired last year. This story demonstrates the initiative that has enabled this ancient Picardy family to remain among the leaders of French industrial society despite poor prospects in their original "metier" and a current legislative environment far from encouraging to private enterprise. Once the decision to switch to yachtbuilding was taken, Henri decided to follow very specific rules, and this has led to the excellent reputation which his products now enjoy. First he determined to opt for quality not quantity; to build only, in his own words, "those boats which I myself would like to buy." To ensure a high standard of construction, first-class, modern facilities would be provided and only designers of good reputation in the type and size of yacht chosen for the market would be employed.

While the tannery provided adequate assembly areas and good joinery shops, it did not have ideal facilities for fiberglass molding. Thus, while the inhabitants of Mouvaux were still celebrating the departure of the olfactory aura of the tannery, Henri planned and completed the construction of a molding factory some 10 kilometers to the north at Neuville adjoining the Belgian frontier post. Expressly designed for fiberglass yachtbuilding, this is a model plant. The ventilation system is vast, moving filtered air under thermostatic control along two overhead ducts from which a series of nozzles project the air downward. These are angled to create circulation and avoid temperature changes at varying levels in the shop. Extractors, some in the form of "elephant trunks," drop down inside the moldings then pass the air back through a large filter. It is almost uncanny to be in a fiberglass boatbuilding plant where the smell of resin is scarcely detected and where the men laying a teak deck have a vacuum tube removing all dust as they go along!

This excellent system is partially attributable to Henri's appreciation of the value of clean, controlled, dust-free air in the attainment of sound laminates, and in part to stringent government factory health regulations. It would be remiss to leave the discussion of factory facilities without mentioning the resin circulation system.

It begins in a 6000-gallon tank from where it is pumped through supply lines to each molding bay. It is in constant circulation through return lines, and its chemical content is under constant supervision. This description is included in this survey because your author firmly believes that recent laminate problems and the vulnerability of hull moldings to osmosis is directly related to the careful control of factory conditions.

The Centurion 47 is the most recent Henri Wauquiez creation. Her role is that of a high-performance yacht that will rate well under PHRF yet provide luxury cruising comfort. Ed Dubois, whose name suggests a fellow Frenchman is, in fact, an Englishman of Huguenot descent whose design office is in Lymington. Henri chose Dubois on the basis of his recent design successes and his willingness to follow through and cooperate with the factory design office. The Dubois-designed *Police Car* won the Admiral's Cup for the Australians in '79, and both *Victory* and *Dragon* were in the British winning team in '81. The Centurion 47 is basically a modification of *Victory* with slightly increased beam. Two models are available—a hull with a deep fin keel for racing, with a draft of 8'6", and a modified longer-keeled cruising version drawing 5'11". The rudder in both is a deep spade carried well aft and supported on a stainless-steel fixed telescopic stock with a top diameter of 4" and ½" wall thickness. To provide added strength, a small skeg runs out under the bustle carrying a stainless steel bearing some 6" in diameter a foot below the through-hull stuffing box. The latter is supported by a reinforced web across the hull. A third bearing at deck level produces an exceedingly robust structure. The rudder itself is a heavy fiberglass blade molded around steel webs which have been welded to the rudder stock inside a foam core to reduce weight.

The hull molding is a solid laminate. The method employed is unusual. To deliver a first-class job on the gel coat and outer layers, preliminary layup is done in two molds which are then brought together, and the process of building up the layers is continued with overlapping layers across the midship section which also serve to strengthen the hull in way of the keel attachment. A reinforcing mold of heavy stringers and floors formed over shaped layers of mat is then dropped into the hull and 11 layers of roving are laid, overlapping across the tops of the floors to give a total laminate of 22 layers on these surfaces. Unidirectional glass is used to provide additional strength in way of the keel and mast-step area. To provide complete dynamic connection between rig and keel, steel plates are bonded into the heavily laminated floor, and stainless steel rods bring the chainplate loads right down to these plates. The 12,800-pound ballast keel has similar horizontal steel plates molded into the lead at three different levels to which are attached the keelbolts—two of 20mm each, seven of 32mm each. One of these fastens directly under the mast step which sits on the same reinforced floor that carries the chainplates. To permit access to this bolt, a 4" aluminum tube is molded into the base of the mast step.

Thus the transfer of forces is beautifully handled. The hull is additionally strengthened by three fore and aft stringers. To ensure perfection of shape, the main bulkheads are positioned and bonded in place before the hull is removed from the mold and while it is still supported by steel beams to which the bulkheads are positioned while bonding takes place.

An unusual bonding technique is employed. The bulkhead edge is drilled with a 1" bit at about 8" centers. When the roving bond is laid, these holes are filled with glass reinforced resin which in turn bonds to the roving on both sides of the bulkhead. Thus, in effect, the bulkheads are both bonded and bolted.

It is these careful applications of good engineering practices that allow Henri Wauquiez to provide a five-year warranty on the structural integrity of his vessels, irrespective of change of ownership. This unusual warranty displays a faith in the quality of construction which this surveyor finds it easy to share. Space does not permit detailed discussion of the deck molding. It is balsa cored, and the Contourkore elements are positioned in a heavy epoxy paste. Where tracks are located, aluminum backing plates are also incorporated in the mold. The hull/deck join is an inbound lip with the continuous aluminum caprail through-bolted at 4" centers. The join is finally glassed over with four layers of mat to ensure total integrity. Before leaving this discussion of hull construction, two other features are worthy of mention. The bronze through-hulls have a serrated external surface and are laminated into the hull during layup. The engine mounting longitudinals are also part of the initial molding process. The bay under the engine is sealed to provide a drip tray and so prevent oil

A completed Centurion 47 hull is given the Gallic water torture at left, to discover any leaks in ports or deck-piercing fastenings. Leaks are not often found; this boat is engineered to a faretheewell, then exhaustively tested in dock and at sea. Henri Wauquiez provides a five-year warranty on the structural integrity of the Centurion 47 which is valid through changes of ownership.

reaching the bilges. The after end is limbered through this space by a glassed-in tube. In the main bilge area, limbering is excellent, culminating in a single low sump in which both manual and electric pump suctions are located. The majority of bilge area is thus available to provide dry storage and battery stowage; the former is looked after by three large plastic removable containers which can be pre-packed, and the latter by sealed batteries stowed in watertight containers.

The external finish of the Centurion 47's hull and deck moldings was excellent; wale stripe, cove stripe and boot-top stripes in the traditional light blue of Wauquiez boats are sprayed into the mold and form part of the gelcoat. Freeboard is high and the sheerline of modest curve; the low coachroof, raked bow and reverse transom follow good contemporary design and suggest both the speed and power developed when this 30,000-pound vessel gets under way.

Turning for a moment to engineering, the engine chosen as standard is the Perkins 4-154, a 62-hp diesel with V-drive transmission turning a two-bladed propeller—a MAX two-bladed propeller being an option. The MAX is an excellent invention; it operates mechanically and has almost paddle-shaped blades with little apparent pitch. When moved from ahead to astern, movement of the blades is effected internally and mechanically. The performance of this propeller left little to be desired; it produced 8½ knots ahead at 2200 rpm, which was cruising speed, not full power. When in neutral, it was automatically feathering. On shifting to astern, power was immediately available and positive. Engine space on the Centurion 47 is well acoustically insulated; immediate access for daily checks is available under the small settee in the master stateroom, and by dropping down into the port cockpit locker one can get into the engine space for servicing. There are two points here that need modification. Firstly, and, it seems, as usual, the acoustically insulated panels on the inside of the lockers cannot be opened without removal of all gear from the locker; secondly, the two engine batteries which lie directly under this access must be covered. At this point it is worthy of note that the finished yacht inspected and sailed at Port Grimaud was the first off the line and thus a number of small glitches were bound to show up as operating experience was gained. The trip to Port Grimaud and the trials conducted there were pleasant experiences; of particular note was the very professional manner in which preparation for and conduct of the inspections and trials was conducted.

Pierre Jean Soler, who does yacht evaluations for the top French yachting magazine "Voiles Et Voiliers" was also present, and we worked together, comparing notes and exchanging views. This international crossfeed was most valuable. Daniel Allisy, well-known photographer and journalist, was along to do the photography and took enormous pains and not a few risks to get good results. Henri Wauquiez was skipper, and we had a really competent crew with Henri Chemineau as sailing master. Henri sailed round the world with Eric Tabarly in *Pen Duick VI*. The final touch was the issue of Wauquiez tee shirts and white foul weather gear to all hands in the interest of good photographic results.

We had two days of sailing, the first in 25 knots of wind and good rough water with a few Mediterranean "square waves," the second in calm seas with 8-10 knots of wind. Even the gods cooperated! Unfortunately Jean was prevented from attending this survey, so I will have to do my best to imagine her impressions later in this report. Returning now to engineering, we will inspect the Perkins installation from the port locker: two nuts on all engine bearers, prop log reasonably accessible under the engine from a "head-down" position, raw-water filter and fuel filters visible and to hand, exhaust "wet box" system neatly installed. The only point picked up here on our joint checklist was the exposed terminals in the locker under the battery charger. These must be boxed in.

The fuel system passed with flying colors. A stainless-steel tank forward on the starboard side for good weight distribution, fuel filler in the anchor locker. A smart trick here is that the tank vent line has a cock in the locker, the handle of which crosses the fuel filler. It is thus impossible to remove the filler cap without first opening the vent line. The tank is then fed without back pressure. When closed, adequate air reaches the tank to permit full fuel flow to the engine through a small pinhole in an anti-syphon device at the top of the vent line. The object of this system is to prevent any danger of fuel loss at extreme angles of heel and is described here as an example of the precise thought which has been put into achieving practical perfection on all systems. Similarly in the plumbing, at both basin drains, a seacock is installed just below the basin with a detour line and electric discharge pump, so that basins can be used at sea without danger of flood back. We did discover that there was a tendency for the forward head to flood if the seacock was left open. This will be looked after by the fitting of a second sea valve on the line, accessible from the head, which can be kept closed except when the system is in use. The two fresh-water tanks were stainless, with a capacity of 142 U.S. gallons. Both had gauges, and the hot water heater was a 12-gallon Raritan with both engine and electrical heating elements.

Based on *Victory*, one of Britain's victorious Admiral's Cup yachts in 1981, the Centurion 47 was designed by Ed Dubois as a high-performance cruising yacht.

There are both racing and cruising below-decks arrangements for this yacht, but both include the sumptuous dining and galley facilities shown here. There are also racing and cruising hull profiles; the cruising version is shown at left.

LOA: 47'
LWL: 38'5"
Beam: 14'6"
Draft: 5'11" (cruising), 8'6" (racing)
Sail Area: 1139 sq. ft. (cruising), 1474 sq. ft. (racing), both with 150% genoa
Ballast: 12,800 pounds
Displacement: 30,000 pounds
Fuel: 95 gallons
Water: 150 gallons
Power: 62-hp Perkins diesel
Spars: aluminum
Hull: hand-layup fiberglass
Designer: Ed Dubois
Builder: Henri Wauquiez, 174 Bd. Carnot, 59420 Mouvaux, France

Refrigeration is an Adler and Barbour electrical system, and the insulation of the fridge/freezer installation is the best I have ever seen. Two bilge pumps are provided—a Henderson manual operated from the helmsman's position and a P.A.R. electric to owner's choice. A Navtec hydraulic system controls boom vang and backstay. Engine instruments are well displayed in a perspex boxed panel to starboard of the helmsman. Engine controls are on the pedestal. As in all good engineering practice, there was an impression of simplicity coupled with top-quality material, along with first-class installation and particular attention paid to access for inspection and service. Coming on deck and starting forward, the anchoring arrangement really works; the leads are right and stainless plates provide protection for the laminate. In the vessel inspected there was an all-chain rode which I would not recommend. In the first place, it puts too much weight forward where it is not wanted; in the second, anchor chains and muddy bottoms produce a filthy mess.

The Lofran 1000-watt electric anchor winch, sunk in the anchor locker and operated by a hand-held, remote-control unit, worked fast and well. It can handle either chain or rope rode. The standard anchor, a 45-pound plough, came up very quickly. I will gloss over deck fittings by simply stating that from eyebolts to hatches they were all of fine quality—with one exception. And they were well-installed, in a layout practical for working the yacht. There are seven Goiot hatches of varying sizes and eight dorade vents to provide very adequate ventilation. There is also an extractor fan at the galley. The exception in quality among the deck fittings, we felt, was the Goiot sliding hatch over the sail locker forward. Henri agrees with these comments and will either call for modification or replace it by one of his own design.

Its faults are firstly clamp handles which stick up and constitute a stinker of a foot hazard for those working the foredeck; secondly, the slide handle is very poor and when closing it nips the fingers. Poor Henri Chemineau provided literal bloody proof of this villainy. I cannot refrain from commenting that far too many yachting subcontractors put gear on the market that has not been adequately tested and proven. Hatch and portlight manufacturers are among the worst offenders. The contrast between the forehatch and Henri's factory-designed companionway hatch was significant. The latter, perspex mounted on stainless steel, and with heavy plastic slides, was excellent. Protected by a small dodger, this hatch was fitted with neat handgrips of stainless steel which were welded across the corners. It led, in turn, to a companionway ladder that was a masterpiece of joinery, its steps curved moldings with non-skid plates on each. A shipwright's pride and joy but, as Henri pointed out, it was heavy!

Before going below, pause a moment in the cockpit. It is a "T" design with a full-sized wheel which runs through a deck recess (an alternate smaller wheel can be shipped for cruising). The sole has a sealed and screwed-down hatch which can be lifted for easy engine removal, and there are two full opening lockers, the starboard especially designed to house an eight-man liferaft. To port is the vast gear and sail locker already discussed. A lazarette under the helmsman's seat provides access to the heavy cable steering gear and yoke with wire strop stops. To port of the helmsman is the propane gas locker which meets all ABYC requirements. At the post-trial "wash-up," when Pierre-Jean and I sat down with Henri to discuss our findings, it was in the cockpit that we had most criticism. We pointed out that there was nowhere to put small gear, spectacles, binoculars, cameras and similar bric-a-brac, and also that the two very large and heavy locker lids required both modification of the hinges and hold-open devices. Both were potential guillotines. Finally, the width between the seats was such that it was not possible to brace oneself satisfactorily.

By the time our meeting was over, all these points had been satisfactorily settled. Footrests were already available for fitting and small gear lockers would be incorporated in the hatch cover modifications.

When the smaller cruising wheel was shipped, extensions could be added to the seats to provide "feet up" comfort. We spent some time discussing the positioning of the instruments. Obviously this is an owner's option, but I found the display in this yacht distracting, with the dials positioned on the after ends of the cockpit seats in the helmsman's "T". This meant that when watching the sail tallies or concentrating on a good downwind course, one had to move one's head and break concentration to check boat speed, etc. This is a good point at which to discuss performance. Although obviously the most important part of this survey report, it would be foolish to indulge in superlatives until the yacht has actually been involved in serious competition. But our initial impression and actual figures obtained were both very satisfactory. When going to windward in fairly steep sea conditions, we started out modestly on day one with two reefs in the main and a working jib, but were obviously under-canvased. After shifting to a No. 2 genoa and shaking out a reef, the Centurion 47 came alive and took off at between 7.5 and 8.2 knots at 32-34 degrees wind angle.

We got the rail down a couple of times, but had to try hard to do it. Her rough-water performance was good; no pounding despite fairly steep waves with an occasional 5'-6' "square one." The wheel was very light, and indeed I would have preferred a little weather helm to give more feel. On the wind the decks remained remarkably dry. We took a couple over the bow but never had water on deck behind the mast. On a spinnaker reach with a radial, we made 9.6-10.2 knots and control remained sweet. Downwind we almost surfed a couple of times. Despite quite heavy quartering seas, one had complete confidence in control. Entering harbor under power was a treat. Control both ahead and astern excellent; indeed, driving astern she ignored even a fair windspeed and went where you wanted. Docking astern was "a piece of cake," as they say in St. Tropez.

Before commenting on the second day of our sea trial, I would like to go below "with Jean" for some comments on the accommodation. This yacht can be purchased in three different modes—a racing version with enlarged sail locker and pipe berth forward, the three-cabin version which we were aboard, and a two-cabin layout. This last would be our choice since it has the master stateroom forward of the saloon and a second large double stateroom aft, each with private head and shower areas. On going below, the first impression is "space." To port below the ladder is the galley, which is almost too large, inasmuch as the cook will require a full-length safety rail and harness to stay in place. One is being provided; the present rail is in place only in front of the stove. The joinery is very good quality, and the corner cupboard has a very pleasing curved door. One of Henri's trademarks is the use of genuine hand-painted glazed tile in his galleys and heads. It is very decorative, and he swears that in the ten years he has used it he has never had crack nor failure. Jean would join me in admiring his taste and the feeling of richness it creates. But while I'd buy it in the heads, I am still conservative enough to prefer smooth counter surfaces and a cutting board in the galley. Henri, charming as always, will smile and fall in with the customer's choice. Jean would give the boat full marks for stowage. Over and above the three plastic bins that can be pre-packed ashore, there are, under the inboard side of the U-shaped settee to starboard, and opening into the passageway, three large

> The construction is among the best I have seen anywhere. Failing accident or total abuse, these vessels will be around for a very long time.

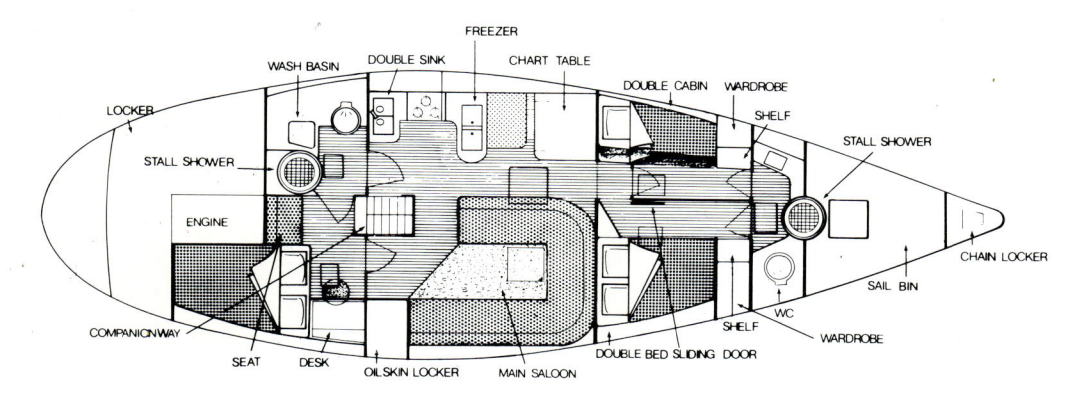

As a cruising boat, the Centurion 47 has the below-decks plan shown here, with big salon/galley area amidships, two guest cabins forward, and an owner's stateroom aft. The forepeak is reserved for sail stowage. In the racing version, there are pipe berths in the space occupied by the guest cabins.

BUSINESS REPLY CARD
FIRST CLASS   PERMIT NO. 1923   NEW YORK N.Y.

POSTAGE WILL BE PAID BY:

Nautical Quarterly
373 Park Avenue South
New York, New York 10016

NO POSTAGE
NECESSARY
IF MAILED
IN THE
UNITED STATES

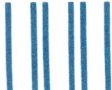

BUSINESS REPLY CARD
FIRST CLASS   PERMIT NO. 1923   NEW YORK N.Y.

POSTAGE WILL BE PAID BY:

Nautical Quarterly
373 Park Avenue South
New York, New York 10016

NO POSTAGE
NECESSARY
IF MAILED
IN THE
UNITED STATES

PLEASE SEND ME THE NAUTICAL QUARTERLY /
SEA CLOUD BROCHURES CHECKED BELOW.
I UNDERSTAND I AM UNDER NO OBLIGATION.

☐ The Caribbean   ☐ The Mediterranean

NAME
_____

ADDRESS
_____

CITY   STATE   ZIP

☐ I would be interested to hear about NQ's plans for a cruise of the China coast in the summer of 1985.

SUBSCRIPTION ORDER FORM

YES! ☐ Please enter my one-year subscription at the annual rate of $60.00. This is a __ new __ renewal subscription.
☐ Please enter the gift subscription(s) as indicated below.

NAME _____
ADDRESS _____
CITY _____ STATE _____ ZIP _____

☐ Payment enclosed   Charge my ☐ MasterCard ☐ Visa ☐ Amex   Acct # _____ Exp. date _____ ☐ Bill me
For faster service on credit card orders...CALL 800-247-2160 TOLL FREE...Anytime.
For orders outside the U.S., add $6.00 per year and remit funds in U.S. dollars. We cannot bill outside the U.S. Expiration date: May 31, 1985.

Send gift subscription to:
NAME _____
ADDRESS _____
CITY _____ STATE _____ ZIP _____
GIFT CARD TO READ FROM: _____
☐ New subscription ☐ Renewal

Send gift subscription to:
NAME _____
ADDRESS _____
CITY _____ STATE _____ ZIP _____
GIFT CARD TO READ FROM: _____
☐ New subscription ☐ Renewal

D43NQXX

SUBSCRIPTION ORDER FORM

YES! ☐ Please enter my one-year subscription at the annual rate of $60.00. This is a __ new __ renewal subscription.
☐ Please enter the gift subscription(s) as indicated below.

NAME _____
ADDRESS _____
CITY _____ STATE _____ ZIP _____

☐ Payment enclosed   Charge my ☐ MasterCard ☐ Visa ☐ Amex   Acct # _____ Exp. date _____ ☐ Bill me
For faster service on credit card orders...CALL 800-247-2160 TOLL FREE...Anytime.
For orders outside the U.S., add $6.00 per year and remit funds in U.S. dollars. We cannot bill outside the U.S. Expiration date: May 31, 1985.

Send gift subscription to:
NAME _____
ADDRESS _____
CITY _____ STATE _____ ZIP _____
GIFT CARD TO READ FROM: _____
☐ New subscription ☐ Renewal

Send gift subscription to:
NAME _____
ADDRESS _____
CITY _____ STATE _____ ZIP _____
GIFT CARD TO READ FROM: _____
☐ New subscription ☐ Renewal

D43NQXX

NO POSTAGE NECESSARY IF MAILED IN THE UNITED STATES

BUSINESS REPLY CARD
FIRST CLASS   PERMIT NO. 1923   NEW YORK N.Y.

POSTAGE WILL BE PAID BY:

Nautical Quarterly Cruise Desk
373 Park Avenue South
New York, New York 10016

provision drawers. In the galley cupboards designed for the crockery there is a neat trick; in the base of each is peg-board with about ⅜" holes. When the crockery is stacked, pegs dropped into these holes fit and hold the stacks in place. The result is safe—and very flexible—stowage for everything. We would recommend bringing the countertops out a couple of inches from the vertical surfaces to compensate for lack of toe spaces underneath, but what is nice is that the galley sole remains flat. A twin sink athwartships, standard four-burner stove with drop-back cover, extractor fan and concealed lighting, and finally the excellent refrigeration already discussed, are all a cook can ask for. He or she can see out, but will have to stand on tiptoe to do it. Forward of the galley on the port side is the navigator's station, and to starboard is the U-shaped settee and large fixed dining table. This layout has the great advantage of fore and aft access throughout the boat with good support on both sides and grab rails within reach.

While discussing the nav station, which is also the electrical control station, a word about the electrical layout. For Europe, a 220 system is provided; for the U.S. a combination of 110 plus 12-volt with six batteries, two alternators on the engine, and a high-capacity battery charger. All circuitry is in conduit and carried above the headliner with access panels at junctions. Every wire is tallied and color-coded. The breaker panel by Bass of Marblehead is unsurpassed, easy to read, every circuit carrying a red tally light and voltmeters and ammeters on both 220 and 12-volt panels. The light fixtures are of high quality and well-positioned. Red courtesy lights at deck level, and the indirect galley lighting, complete the "everything has been thought of" impression. The electronic package is the owner's option, and in this case SATNAV was in and working. The layout of instruments and book racks around the full-size chart table, with a comfortable navigation seat, was all that a fussy navigator could ask for. One of the advantages is that he doesn't get smothered when the spinnaker comes flowing down the companionway during a "mad-flap" sail change. Forward of the saloon on the port side is an upper and lower double, on the starboard a double-berth cabin. Both cabins have separate access to the head compartment forward. The door to the sail locker will need heavier clamps, we think; the pressure of sails, plus foredeck gorillas jumping on them, will burst the current bolting arrangement. This "sail inventory" business is, in the mind of a cruising sailor and a racing sailor from yesteryear like myself, a pest. We had seven sails aboard which just about filled the sail locker forward and the port cockpit locker. The racing version of this yacht, with its additional space forward between pipe berths, should solve this problem (for those whose sail inventories run to the ridiculous). Stuffing wet sails into a luxuriously appointed saloon seems somewhat profane.

Aft, the master stateroom has a very adequate double berth with feet aft and headboard to catch the pillows, a hanging locker to starboard, a seat and a vanity table with well-sloped mirror and pull-out stool. A clever touch is that this vanity stool can shift into the saloon where it drops into a prepared slot to provide an extra seat at the head of the table. The head is commodious and well laid out with a door behind the shower leading through into the port locker. An opening port in the stateroom gives access to the cockpit.

Finally back on deck for a look at the rig. Three spreaders and running backstays, forestay, babystay, and uppers of 12 mm (.47"), 14 mm lowers (.55"), and 8 mm (.31") intermediates, coupled to the chainplate system already described, provide a very powerful rig. An outfit of 13 Lewmar winches, in descending order from the two-speed No. 65 self-tailing primaries, certainly covered all working requirements. And despite the profusion of back-up cleats and clam cleats, the deck layout was orderly and practical.

As Henri Wauquiez provides excellent specifications and equipment lists, plus a good "Owner's Manual," I will not go into further detail. The real purpose of these survey reports is to provide the reader with an overview of the construction and performance of the yacht under study. In the interest of providing more than the nuts & bolts of a technical survey report, facts are threaded to opinions and subjects are covered in varying order in the hope that the end result will be a good general impression. Everyone has their own tastes; each must choose his own. In the case of the Centurion 47, however, it is very clear that Henri Wauquiez, Ed Dubois and those who have worked with them to produce this yacht have come up with an outstanding vessel. The construction is among the best I have seen anywhere. Failing accident or total abuse, these vessels will be around for a very long time. There is no planned obsolescence here. The Centurion 47 is no "skinned-out" *Police Car*, but the performance is very much there. With the choice of a slightly reduced rig available on the cruising option, coupled with reduced keel draft, and with the special racing interior at the other end of the scale, the Centurion 47 series can provide for a variety of tastes. An investment in this yacht should be good for the long haul.

NAUTICAL QUARTERLY, THE DREAM-MAKER, CAN ALSO MAKE DREAMS COME TRUE.

**Announcing:
Two Exceptional Cruises Aboard the Legendary *Sea Cloud***

(Use the adjoining reply card to request a fully descriptive brochure for either or both cruises!)

For 1985, we have reserved cabins for Nautical Quarterly readers aboard Sea Cloud, the world's largest sailing yacht, for voyages in two of the world's greatest cruising grounds—the Leeward Islands and the Mediterranean.

Built as a yacht by E.F. Hutton, founder of the brokerage firm, and his wife Marjorie Merriweather Post, Sea Cloud has been restored and maintained as perhaps the most lavish sailing yacht afloat. Carrying a maximum of 75 passengers with a crew of 60, she sails with elegance, indeed splendor, and offers an unparalleled cruise experience.

We invite you to send for the brochures that describe these cruises in detail.

The Caribbean—March 9-16, 1985

Planned for the Caribbean's most ideal time of year from the sailor's point of view, this cruise embarks at Antigua on March 2nd and touches at the fabled islands of St. Martin, Saba, Martinique, Isles des Saintes, and Peter Island in the British Virgins.

Each luxurious cabin is air-conditioned for individual comfort, and you will enjoy excellent cuisine, and friendly, fit-for-a-king service while sailing the turquoise seas of Columbus and Sir Francis Drake on this magnificent vessel.

The Mediterranean—June 2-17, 1985

This unique cruise ranges from a port of Rome (Civitavecchia) to the port of Athens (Piraeus)! On the western part of the voyage, we will pay visits to the romantic islands of Ischia and Capri, Taormina on Sicily, and Malta. There will be a layover at Gallipoli on the heel of Italy before the two-day passage to the Aegean, where landfall will be made at Iraklion on Crete. We will visit Santorini, Mykonos and Patmos before disembarking at Piraeus.

Special tours of these ancient and historic islands have been arranged that will surprise even the most inveterate of Nautical Quarterly's experienced travelers. The month of June is considered the most auspicious weatherwise, prior to le mistral and the Aegean's meltemi!

Colorful brochures for leisurely browsing

Send for the brochures now. Only 36 fortunate NQ couples can be accommodated, so mail the adjoining reply card just as quickly as possible.

A GIFT FOR ALL SEASONS.
A GIFT FOR ALL REASONS.

Surely *you* have a reason to honor someone with NAUTICAL QUARTERLY today.

For instance, we've filled gift orders from:

A sailor with a bad back to his orthopedic surgeon
(a fellow sailor)

A chairman of a board, at Christmas, to four fellow directors
(two who sail, two who power)

A teen-age daughter to her father, on his birthday

A yacht club prize committee chairman to his entire
junior sailing membership

A wife who was desperate, to her husband who (now) has everything

A power-yacht broker to customers who rely on him
for any boat over 30 feet

A guest at a boat christening, whose invitation said
"no presents please"

A new wooden-boat owner to the craftsman who built her

The owner of a Whitbread Race contender to his crew, in Portsmouth

A sailmaker to his winning customers, year in and year out

A yachtsman to his ad agency's art director,
celebrating a new campaign

NAUTICAL QUARTERLY has been honored by the magazine industry with its highest award for design, one of the National Magazine Awards presented by the American Society of Magazine Editors, the citation noting that "the editorial ideas are presented with purity, freshness and consistency of style that is all too rare." This recognition by our peers substantiates your good taste and suggests that NQ would be an impeccable gift for people *you* want to honor.

Fife of Fairlie was a legend in the yachting world until the start of the Second World War, and the name is recalled today as synonymous with elegant racing or cruising yachts, and associated with two challenges for the America's Cup. Yachtsmen have heard the name, and have admired yachts still sailing which were designed and built in that little town on the Firth of Clyde, for the Fifes built well. But few realize that there were three generations of William Fifes whose work stretched from the beginning of the 19th century into the middle of the 20th. There was also a nephew, Robert Balderston Fife, who carried on the tradition during the 1920s and 1930s. □ The Fifes did not have a family chronicler in the way that L. Francis Herreshoff served to record and publicize the lives and accomplishments of his forbears, and it is now difficult to discover the details of their personal lives. All four of them were creative and diligent workers in the design and construction of great yachts and small craft, and all possessed that educated and courteous conduct which is so typical of Scots, in and out of business. They were modest but gifted men, and what they have left us is the record of their achievements over more than a hundred years of yacht racing, and some few yachts which bespeak their genius and their workmanship.

Fairlie is a small town on the coast of the county of Ayrshire, on the southeast shore of the Firth of Clyde and about 25 miles from Glasgow. At the beginning of the 19th century it was a small and isolated village off which was an exposed anchorage, an unlikely place for the site of a yachtbuilding yard whose ways would launch legendary vessels. The geography remained the same for 140 years, of course, and considerable ingenuity was required to launch large yachts off a foreshore that shelved away gradually and had little depth of water even at high tide. Sir Thomas Lipton's 23 Meter *Shamrock*, as an example, because of her draft of 13', was launched from the Fairlie foreshore in 1908 on a pontoon, which was sunk under her when she had been towed out to sufficient depth.

In this little place far removed from the beginnings of yachting in southeastern and southern England in the late 18th century, the first William Fife, who was born in 1775, apprenticed with his father as a wheelwright. In those days, ships sometimes anchored for shelter or were windbound in the roadstead off Fairlie, and the wheelwright's son built a rowing boat for himself to examine the ships more closely and to fully enjoy the waterside. The form and finish of this boat attracted attention, and a good offer resulted in its sale. The boy built another one with the same result. A buyer for a third boat turned up before she was planked. Thus the first William Fife became a boatbuilder, although his father, it is said, did not approve. Little is known of his early output, much of which was probably local fishing skiffs—open boats of about 19', rigged with a single dipping lugsail, and fast for their size. It is likely that he ventured into building some of the cutter-rigged trading smacks which then carried cargo to and from the many isolated communities on the Firth of Clyde and to the isles and coasts of western Scotland. William Fife leased his bit of foreshore from the Kelbourne Castle estate of the Earl of Glasgow, his father's employer. The Earl became so interested in the boatbuilding enterprise that he charged only a token rent of a shilling a year, but the independent young Scot asked for this to be increased, and so the Earl charged him a full pound to satisfy his pride.

When we think of the Fifes we think of the third William Fife, who was born in 1857 and died in 1944 at a time when no yachts had been built in his yard for four years. His long career had stretched from the lean, oversparred cutters and yawls of the 1870s to the seaworthy offshore yachts of the late 1930s, making him the unquestioned patriarch of yacht design and construction in Britain and the world. No one else had worked as long and with such integrity as had this William Fife, and the yachts built at Fairlie in his 87 years were among the finest in the world.

But the Fifes were a yachtbuilding family almost since the beginning. Early in the 19th century the sport had spread to the Clyde from the south and east coasts of England; industrialists were building empires in Glasgow and were looking to the Clyde for leisure and sport, and they were joined by some of the long-established Scottish aristocracy. William Fife built several early yachts for them, including the 50-ton cutter *Lamlash*, the first flagship of the Royal Northern Yacht Club, launched in 1812, and the cutter *Gleam*, fastest of the contemporary Clyde yachts. *Lamlash* was built for James Hamilton, the Commodore of the RNYC, and she was the first Scottish-owned yacht to cruise to the Mediterranean. She was probably about 60′ long on deck, with a plumb stem and a short counter stern, generally resembling a refined version of the trading and fishing smacks of the time, and she must have been a considerable venture for the young boatbuilder. Other yacht commissions came along soon enough, and the little yard even built a steam vessel. The 70-ton paddle steamer *Industry* was laid down on the Fairlie foreshore in 1814, and she was built so well that she remained in service until nearly 1890. Her original side-lever type steam engine, with its spur-wheel gearing, was set up in Kelvinside Park in Glasgow when she was broken up.

The first William Fife designed his vessels at first by carving models, but when yacht owner James Hill told him of a book, *Steele's Naval Architecture*, he sent to London for a copy and studied it thoroughly. He designed and built perhaps a dozen little luggers of about 19′-23′ each year for the local herring fishery, at about £50 each, and he continued to build yachts for the gentry and for the sporting industrialists. He became an excellent draftsman, although self-taught, and he always wished vessels of his design to be "bonnie."

> The first William Fife designed his vessels at first by carving models, but when yacht owner James Hill told him of a book, *Steele's Naval Architecture*, he sent to London for a copy and studied it thoroughly.

In 1835, the first William Fife's son, another William, started an apprenticeship at Fairlie when he was 13 years old. This second William Fife was a robust boy who had considerable physical strength, along with that dogged endurance typical of his race. He also had his father's gift for design and his capacity for hard work. By 1839, when he was 17, the second William Fife took over management of the yard; he was draftsman, foreman and clerk, and when not at these tasks it was said of him that he "wrought as much at the boat side and the bench as any other at the yard."

He also seems to have been stubborn. A schooner of his design was laid down as a "spec" yacht and stood in the stocks for three years awaiting a buyer. Eventually a firm offer came, but the owner asked Fife to raise the bulwarks to a height of 3′ instead of the 15″ or so that was common in a hull of that size. Fife said, "No, I canna do it. I've kept her a long time, and I'm anxious to get rid of her; but I'll keep her a long time yet rather than make a cart of her at the finish." The owner finally accepted the existing bulwarks as "safe" and bought her. After many years of successful cruising, she was sold to the Queen of Portugal to continue a long career.

For more than 40 years, until 1881, the second William Fife designed and built a fleet of yachts, many of which were notable racers. His most successful included *Stella*, *Cymba*, *Cinderella*, *Surge*, *Oithona*, *Torch*, *Kilmeny*,

Scenes from Fairlie in the summer of 1983 are shown on this and previous pages. The sheds of the old yard are shown on page 102 accompanied by the church and the stone houses of the little town. Also to be seen is the shallow foreshore with the tide out. It is remarkable that vessels as large as 23-Meter yachts were launched here, and a tribute to such legendary Scottish qualities as ingenuity, endurance and stubborn will. A marine railway was built on pilings out to deeper water in the old days, and some yachts were floated out on pontoons as well. The yacht shown here, seen close to the sheds on page 102, was worked out to a place where the tide would float her on baulks of timber. The work was done by main force, and one of the men who put his shoulder to it was Archie Macmillan, shown on page 103 at more delicate work. The yard is now managed by Archie Macmillan as a service facility.

One of the prettiest of the smaller Fife yachts is *Merry Dancer,* shown here with a deep reef in her main on her way out into the English Channel with a new owner and a delivery crew aboard. She was built in 1938 as one of the fast cruiser/handicap-racer/offshore-racer yachts of approximately 35′ waterline length that were encouraged by British offshore-racing rules just before and just after World War II. *Merry Dancer* was built to the usual high standards of the Fife yard, with mahogany planking over oak frames fastened with copper rivets, and with laid teak decks and teak house structure and trim. Her planking is joined together with wedges fitted and glued into the seams, as well as fastened to the frames, which gives the hull an extra bit of integrity and a perfectly smooth surface with no plank seams showing.

Fiona, and *Neva. Stella* was a cutter designed in 1848 for the flourishing 40-ton class, and her racing success under Clyde yachtsman Hugh Morris Lang and professional skipper Robert McKirdy established her builder's reputation. *Cymba,* built on speculation, was all but unbeatable in her class for two seasons. The success of the Fifes, father and son, is all the more remarkable when it is realized that when the first William Fife began to build boats there was not a yacht on the Clyde and Scotland was a poor country until industry brought wealth to a few. But despite the reputation of the second William in the north, he was little known in the fashionable centers of yachting in England.

This began to change with the long career of *Fiona,* built in 1865 for a Liverpool merchant whose business faltered before he could take delivery. She had two other owners in quick succession, and the last, Samuel Boucher, appointed John Houston of the Clydeside town of Largs as skipper. For ten years, Boucher and Houston raced *Fiona,* and for eight of them she was all but unbeatable. She was a typical racing cutter of the time: 75′ long x 15′8″ beam, and with 11′10″ draft; a hull with plumb stem and counter stern; mast 44′5″ deck to hounds; boom 60′; gaff 38′; bowsprit 34′ outboard; topmast 38′; area of mainsail, staysail and jib 3720 square feet.

After 1874, *Fiona* became a cruiser, and in 1898 she was bought by Scottish yachtsman H. M. Rait, who had an obsession to own her. She was thoroughly refitted and entered in handicap racing with Captain Fred Pearman of Rowhedge, Essex, in charge, and with a crew from the River Colne. Captain Pearman and *Fiona* became particularly well known for fast performances in the early races from Dover to the island of Heligoland for a cup given by the German Emperor. *Fiona* won this cup in 1900, and her owner was delighted with the success of this racing yacht that was then 40 years old. Rait loved to see her go. With everything straining in strong winds and the topmast threatening to break at any moment, he would stand by Captain Pearman on the spray-swept deck, proudly taking in the bend of the topmast and the roaring wake, and would reply to the skipper's warning glance, "Never mind, Frederick—let it go; God bless the old *Fiona*!" At Kiel, the Emperor came aboard to see the men who had won his cup, and was impressed with these wool-capped giants from Essex and their grand old yacht. *Fiona* continued to win offshore events and other handicap races of the time until 1906 when her owner died and she was afterward broken up.

By the 1870s, yachting on the Clyde was flourishing, and Scottish yachtsmen were determined to have a crack at the flyers from the south of England. Experienced crews were a problem, however, for most of Scotland's best racing hands were aboard *Fiona* and a few other noted northern racers. National pride was foregone, however, and word went to the south for skippers and hands. On the River Colne in Essex, where racing and cruising yachts had been built and manned since the 1780s, there was a new generation eager to make their racing reputations with new yachts, and many of these young men entrained for the north to stand by the new racers being launched by Reid at Paisley and by Fife and by his former employee Hugh Boag at Fairlie. The debt the reputations of Fife, Watson, Mylne, Reid and other Scottish designers owed to these soft-spoken Essex men is now mostly forgotten, but was freely acknowledged in their day when yachting correspondents wrote of the Clyde racers being "manned by smart and powerful English crews."

In this atmosphere of expanding sport, the second William Fife designed and built a succession of outstanding yachts for cruising and racing, and in 1876 he had the pleasure of seeing his son, the third of the Williams, design his first yacht at the age of 19. One of the great Fife yachts of the 1870s was a 60-ton cutter that was begun on speculation and bought while on the stocks by Scottish businessman Holmes Kerr, who was determined to challenge the big class with her. He engaged Captain Lemon Cranfield of Rowhedge, Essex, to sail his new *Neva* with a crew of Rowhedge men, and they made her a legend for speed all around the coast. During the four seasons 1874-1877, *Neva* sailed in 95 races and won 57 prizes worth a total of £3525, besides almost wrecking the 60-ton class with her success. Lemon Cranfield went on to become one of the greatest professional racing skippers of all time.

Another long-lived Fife yacht was *Blood Hound*, owned in her first few seasons by the Marquis of Ailsa and sailed successfully by Captain Ben Harris of Itchen, Southampton. *Blood Hound* was outclassed in 40-ton racing in the mid-1870s and became a cruiser. But she was bought back by the Marquis of Ailsa in 1909 and was completely refitted and altered, her forefoot being cut away to reduce wetted surface, her ballast being placed in an external lead keel, and her rig modernized. She emerged in the rather startled large-handicap class under Captain Ben Chaplin of Brightlingsea, Essex, with a crew from the Colne, and she proceeded to win 143 prizes in 217 races before World War I.

When the third William Fife took up yacht design, he began with a 28' cutter of 5 tons named *Clio*, which was raced with his uncle, Allan Fife, at the tiller. Allan had the reputation of being the best amateur on the Clyde in the 1870s. *Clio* was followed by another 5-tonner named *Camellia*, and a third, *Cyprus*, designed for himself. His father, meanwhile, was at the height of his powers, and the son determined to obtain wider experience at one of the Clyde's shipbuilding yards. He worked in the drawing office of J. Fullerton at Paisley on the design and fabrication planning of iron and steel commercial vessels, familiarizing himself with metal, which was then increasingly being used in yachtbuilding for frame members, keels, floors, deck beams, etc., and soon would be used for masts and spars in large yachts.

The third William, who came to be known as "William Fife, Jr.," began to build his reputation with two large yachts designed for his father's yard while he was still at Fullerton's—the 40-ton *Sleuth Hound*, designed for the Marquis of Ailsa, and another 40-tonner, *Annasona*. *Sleuth Hound* won the Albert Cup in 1881, a Queen's Cup in 1882 and 1883, and many other prizes. In 1881, the second William Fife, then 60 years old, stopped designing yachts and the third William began in earnest. He was soon a rising international name in yacht design, and unlike his rivals, George L. Watson of Glasgow and Alexander Richardson of Liverpool, he had the advantage of an old established family tradition and a yard to back it.

For a time, in fact, he had two yards to back it. About 1881, the Marquis of Ailsa established a boatyard near his home at Culzean Castle, and asked William Fife, Jr. to become its manager. The new firm was named the Culzean Ship Building and Engineering Company, and was equipped for steel construction as well as wood. Notable yachts built at Culzean included the 345-ton steel barquentine-rigged yacht *Black Pearl*, a 150' vessel with steam auxiliary power that was well-known in British yachting for many years before being sold to an American, and the 110' steam yacht *Cassandra*. One of the few racing yachts built at Culzean was the Fife-designed cutter *Clara*, launched in 1884 for the popular 20-ton class to the order of J.G. Clark. Of composite construction, at which Fife was able to shine after his experience at Fullerton's, *Clara* was typical of the extreme form which the British racing rules of the time had forced on designers. Her overall length was 63'9", with 52'9" on the waterline, but her maximum beam was only 9'9". She drew 9'6" aft, and was of 36.5 tons displacement, of which 21.9 tons were lead ballast.

In 1885, she was sold to an English lawyer named Charles Sweet, who had connections with an American lawyer named Charles Tweed. They became joint owners and appointed Captain John Barr of Greenock as skipper to race her in the U.S. *Clara* brought the renowned America's Cup skipper Charlie Barr, John Barr's young half-brother, to America, and she became almost unbeatable in the American 55' class. In 1881, the Watson-designed 10-tonner *Madge* had come to America, and her racing success started a craze for British cutters among some American yachtsmen. *Clara*'s success further encouraged the "cutter cranks," who were partisans of keelboats in reaction to the prevalent American racing yachts of the time, which were shallow and often extreme centerboard boats.

Another American success for Fife was *Minerva*, a cutter of 40' waterline length designed for Charles Tweed in 1888. Fife was free to produce the design as he pleased so long as she was fast; the paradox was that Tweed did not intend to race her, he just wanted a fast cruiser of a modified British cutter type. *Minerva* was a keel yacht of greater beam than was then usual in British racing, with moderate displacement and with a counter stern and clipper bow. Her rating was by waterline length instead of the established British method of length on deck, which had resulted in the plumb stem characteristic of British racers, to gain maximum waterline length. The era of the plumb-stem cutter would be over that year with the introduction of a new British rating rule.

Minerva was sailed across the Atlantic by young Captain Charles Barr, and served as a cruiser for a time. But due to damage to another yacht before a regatta in the season of 1888, she was "borrowed" by a racing crew and won handsomely over yachts designed by Burgess and Gardner, America's leading designers of the time. She continued this success during 1889 and 1890, and became the top boat of the 40' waterline class.

There is insufficient space here to detail the many racing yachts, from 40-raters to 5-raters, designed and built by the third William Fife in the late 1880s and 1890s, as well as other vessels from rowing gigs to steam yachts. Like his father and grandfather, he lived at Fairlie. He had limited spare time and used it in sailing a small yacht for day-cruising about the Clyde, sometimes racing. For several years he owned the 4-ton sloop *May*, which he had designed and had the yard build in 1894. He remained a bachelor all his life, and although absorbed in his work he was a genial man and well-liked.

In 1892-3, four of the largest class of racing cutters were built—the Watson-designed *Britannia* for the Prince of Wales; *Satanita*, designed by Joseph Soper for A.D. Clarke; the Watson-designed *Valkyrie II* for the Earl of Dunraven; and *Calluna*, designed by Fife and built by Inglis of Glasgow for Peter Donaldson. *Calluna* was sailed by Captain Archie Hogarth, an Ayrshire native who had sailed two smaller Fife racers with great success. The combination of a designer and a skipper who were comparatively inexperienced in big-class racing yachts inevitably resulted in *Calluna* being bottom of the class, despite many alterations to trim, gear and sails. But they were learning with

> In 1898, grocery magnate Thomas Lipton came to Fife for a racing cutter which would be the first of his *Shamrocks*. He told William, "Now, Fife, I haven't money to burn; but, if it will make her a second faster, shovel on the notes."

this boat, and both Fife and Hogarth were to reach success with similar giant yachts in a few years. Fife's 130' cutter *Ailsa*, built two years later, won many races in England and on the Riviera, and sailed in the transatlantic race of 1905 under yawl rig.

In 1898, grocery magnate Thomas Lipton came to Fife for a racing cutter which would be the first of his *Shamrocks* to challenge for the America's Cup. He told William, "Now, Fife, I haven't money to burn; but, if it will make her a second faster, shovel on the notes." *Shamrock*, which generally resembled a more extreme version of *Ailsa*, was 128' overall, 89'8" on the waterline, 25' beam and 20'3" draft. The hull was flat-sheered and beamy, with long overhangs, and the keel was a deep fin with considerable rake to the rudder stock at its after end. Sail area was 13,492 square feet in mainsail, staysail, No. 1 jib and yard topsail. She was built on the Thames by John I. Thornycroft with a manganese bronze bottom, aluminum topsides, and spars of steel.

Big racing yachts were becoming too extreme at the end of the 'nineties, and had a competitive life of only two or three seasons before being outclassed. They were of little use as cruisers. William Fife deplored this style of yacht, which had been developing since 1893-4, and which produced the dullest big-class racing season anyone could remember in 1898. In 1900 there was no British big-class racing at all, and the new Watson racing yawl *Kariad* had to go to Kiel to find some racing against the German Emperor's yawl *Meteor II*. By 1901, the 52' class had been reduced to three new yachts. Although the war in South Africa was blamed for this state of affairs, the problem was the yachts themselves, and there began to be talk of a new rating rule.

At the end of 1901, the health of the elder William Fife broke down. He died in January, 1902, aged 80, the patriarch of British yachtbuilders and designers. Before he died he had the pleasure of knowing that his son had secured a commission to design another large racing yacht, a schooner this time, for Cecil Quentin, who had owned handicap-class yachts for several years. The new boat was the 130' *Cicely*, which did well against the German Emperor's new schooner *Meteor III* in the seasons of 1902 and 1903. She was followed in 1904 by the 110' schooner *Suzanne*, designed for a German owner and campaigned successfully until 1914, and again in the early 'twenties.

During the winter of 1902-03, William Fife designed the large racing cutter *Shamrock III* for Sir Thomas Lipton to challenge the enormous Herreshoff-designed *Reliance* for the America's Cup. She was a graceful yacht 134'6" overall, 89'10" on the waterline, 25' beam and 19'11" draft. Sail area was 13,851 sq. ft. and displacement was 165.5 tons. She was built of mild steel with an aluminum deck by William Denny and Brothers at Dumbarton, and her specially designed and made deck and rigging fittings, and the details of her hull, rig and gear, were no less carefully thought-out than those of her rival, although Fife's work does not nowadays receive the same adulation.

Besides designing and supervising the building of numbers of yachts, William Fife spent time trying to further the work of framing a new rating rule for racing yachts. He was keen to encourage fast, graceful and useful yachts rather than the misshapen, rule-engendered, potentially prizewinning, but ugly yachts then in vogue. There was an echo of his father's refusal to raise a yacht's bulwarks in this. Along with Charles Nicholson and other designers, he had the pleasure of seeing this work completed in 1906 when the new International Rule of Rating was introduced.

Of the first three large racing yachts designed to this rule, two were Fife designs, the attractive cutters *White Heather II* of 1907 and Sir Thomas Lipton's *Shamrock,* launched the following season and always referred to by the yacht captains and crews as "*Shamrock* 23 Meter" to distinguish her from the five other *Shamrocks* which were challengers for the America's Cup. This *Shamrock* was perhaps William Fife's most

One of only a few yachts built by the Fairlie yard after World War II is *Navara II*, a lovely double-ender designed by Archie Macmillan for himself. She was built for the 8 Meter International Cruiser/Racer class, a special formula for yachts which raced on the Clyde beginning in 1950. Yachts were built for this class until 1967 by several Clyde yards to designs by Robb, Morris, Lorimer and McGruer, but only Archie Macmillan's work had this graceful canoe stern in the Fife tradition of the 1930s. Another Fife tradition to be seen on this yacht and on many others is the cove stripe with stylized dragon's head and tail in gold and red. This is a decoration which has distinguished many Fife-built yachts since the 1890s, when it first appeared on racing yachts, appropriately named *Dragon*, built for Scottish yachtsman F.C. Hill.

successful racing yacht. She consistently won prizes from 1908 until she was outclassed by the Bermudian-rigged cutters in 1929. The 23-Meter yachts were fast but wet, despite their reasonable freeboard, but were seaworthy for coastwise passagemaking and short sea crossings, and were admired for this ability by contemporary American observers. They set almost 10,000 square feet without the spinnaker or big jib topsail, shipped a crew of 22, and cost about £12,000 fitted-out, which was a tremendous sum in those days.

William Fife designed many successful International-Rule yachts in the years before the First World War, especially 15-Meter yachts, and he also produced a few motor vessels, but in 1910 he designed a yacht that appeared to be all that a large racing schooner should be and yet proved to be the greatest disappointment of his career. The new schooner *Waterwitch* was launched early in 1911 to race against the American *Westward* and the German yachts *Meteor* and *Germania* in the "A" class, above the 23-Meter rating. Her owner was G. Gordon Whitaker, who had owned the attractive Fife-designed schooner *Cicely,* which had been launched in 1902. *Waterwitch* did not race until the great International Regatta off Ryde, Isle of Wight, in July of 1911, organized to celebrate the coronation of King George V. When she met the two German schooners (*Westward* was no longer in England) she was rapidly left behind by her slightly larger but older rivals, and journalist Herbert Reiach wrote: "It was already known that something was amiss with *Waterwitch,* Britain's hope. Evidently she requires additional sail to drive her, and the bow and stern waves suggest that she is big. Below water she is clean, but the ends appear to be too much for the moderate sail. *Waterwitch* is but another example of the fascinating uncertainty of yacht designing..."

During the winter of 1911-12 she was extensively altered and came out in 1912 with increased sail area, but she was beaten worse than before. Her skipper and crew were as dismayed as Fife, and the owner was furious. After a few races he ordered her to be hauled out. All the fittings and gear, masts, spars, sails and rigging were removed, and the hull, only 15 months old, was broken up. Whitaker put her rig and fittings into a new schooner designed by Charles Nicholson with instructions that she must be capable of beating any other racing schooner in the world. The result was *Margherita,* which beat her German rivals handily with the same captain and crew that had failed with *Waterwitch.*

This contretemps caused Fife considerable worry, and it affected his prospects in the design of big-class racers for many years. But his other racers were upholding the family tradition in classes from little 6 Meters to 23-Meter cutters. And the past, of course, was glorious history. The output of yachts designed and built by the Fife family before 1914 was considerable. Lloyd's Register of Yachts for 1914 lists 308 Fife yachts in commission, ranging from the 4-ton *Susu* to the 261-ton *Ailsa*.

There was little demand for the services of yachtbuilders in a war which rapidly became dominated by machines, but William Fife and Son built a large number of small motor craft and ship's boats for the Royal Navy during the First World War. And very quickly after the war, in late 1919, Fife received a pleasing commission from Charles Johnson to design and build a large cutter to race in the large handicap class, which represented the "big class" of the early 1920s, and also to serve for cruising. This was *Moonbeam*—95′ overall, 60′ waterline length, 16′ beam and 12′ draft. Sail area was 4261 square feet in a cutter rig. She represented, in essentials, the type of moderately large racing yacht which many owners desired. Although more large racing yachts were to be built in Britain and in the U.S., yachtsmen in both countries knew that something smaller would be as much fun to race and yet be much less expensive to build, sail and maintain. There was also a surge of interest in the early 'twenties in boats for smaller-class racing.

At this time, William Fife took into partnership his nephew, Robert Balderston Fife, and from the 12 Meter *Vanity* of 1923 onwards he exerted an increasing influence in the family firm. The 1920s saw a virtual fleet of 6 Meters launched at Fairlie, so much so that they were jokingly referred to as "the Fife class" on the Clyde and the Solent. At Cowes one regatta week, William Fife was watching a dozen sixes come to the line and asked a bystander, with typical Scottish directness, "Let me look at your programme; my boats are so alike I can't tell one from another."

During the period 1919-1939, the two Fifes' main rivals were Charles Nicholson, whose yachts were generally built at the family yard of Camper & Nicholson at Gosport, and Alfred Mylne of Glasgow, whose company operated a yard at Port Bannatyne, Rothesay, and built at other Clyde yards, including Fife's. Their rivalry was particularly keen in 12 Meters during the 1920s and 1930s. Although the big classes then dominated the public, and to some extent, the yachting press, the finest sport was provided by the twelves, which were then seaworthy and habitable yachts between 62′ and 72′ with accommodations for a professional crew of four and an owner's party of perhaps three. They could and did make passages around the coast under sail from regatta to regatta, anywhere from Harwich in the east to the Clyde in the west, with occasional dashes across the Channel to race at Deauville and LeHavre. Some even ventured north to the Baltic regattas.

The Fifes designed and built three twelves in succession for Clyde shipbuilder Arthur Connell—*Zinita* in 1927, *Zoraida* in 1932, and *Zelita* in 1933. The first of these was relatively successful, but the final two were disappointments, especially *Zelita*, which was discarded after one losing season. Arthur Connell forsook Fife and ordered a new twelve from Nicholson, the successful *Westra*. How much blame attached to the boats, their designers and builders? Probably a good deal, as Connell was an experienced racing helmsman, and he had in Captain William Wadley and a good crew from Rowhedge, Essex, an able professional complement supplemented by keen and experienced amateurs. This sequence of failed boats must have been almost as great a blow to the Fifes as the *Waterwitch* fiasco of 20 years before.

But there were successes, among them *Vanity V*, a new twelve built for John R. Paine in 1936, which was a consistent prizewinner. John R. Paine was known to the racing fraternity as "Fiddler" Paine for his fondness for playing the violin. He was a fine amateur helmsman, but his musical efforts often annoyed his professional crew, only a few feet away in the foc's'le and separated from the violinist by nothing but a thin wooden bulkhead.

In addition to the Meter yachts of the International Rule, and the cruising yachts which campaigned in day races of 40 miles or so and were vessels of undoubted elegance and speed, a new style of yacht came along in the mid-1920s in response to a new form of the sport—ocean racing. Many younger sailing men were keen to race in what were usually smallish yachts, with mainly amateur crews, and over much longer coastwise courses or across the North Sea, the English Channel, and into the Baltic, in the early 1920s, as their contemporaries were doing in America, Canada, Australia and New Zealand. At first these yachts were a mixture of cruisers and ex-racers, but from the mid-'twenties what began to evolve was a new style of yacht, more fitted for offshore sailing at sustained speed. This was given impetus by the founding in Britain of the Ocean Racing Club after the first race around Fastnet Rock in 1925. A rating rule was established, and many of the yachts designed and built in Britain for racing offshore were amongst the most seamanlike ever launched.

William Fife must have rejoiced in the breed. Both he and R. Balderston Fife were keenly interested in the emergence of this new form of yacht racing, and in 1925 the two Fifes jointly designed the 75′ Bermudian cutter *Hallowe'en* for J. F. N. Baxendale as a fast cruiser which would occasionally race offshore. Her owner particularly wished to win the Fastnet race with her. Her Bermudian rig caused a flutter amongst the offshore fraternity, whose yachts were then largely gaff-rigged, but with a smart professional crew under Jack Arnold of Basham, Sussex, backed by the owner and his family and friends as good amateurs, *Hallowe'en* went well and finished the dash to Fastnet Rock and back to Plymouth in 3 days, 19 hours, a new record time. She finished third on handicap to Britain's *Ilex*. She was sold to a Norwegian and renamed *Magda III*, and afterwards became a famous ocean racer in America as *Cotton Blossom IV*, owned and campaigned by Walter Wheeler. She is still sailing almost 60 years after her launching.

The 1930s saw a great flowering of

yachtbuilding in Britain, and the quality of most of the vessels built has never been excelled. In the shadow of severe economic depression and a growing threat of war in Europe, it seemed that British yachtsmen were determined to enjoy their sport to the full. The Fifes designed 8-Meter boats as well as twelves, and their designs for *Caryl* (1929), *Finola* (1930), *Saskia* (1931), *Carron II* (1935) and *Felma* (1937) vindicated their ability to produce a beautiful yacht which was also fast. The Nicholson designs *Sagitta*, *Wye*, *Reality*, *Rosa*, and *Cedora* gave Fife boats a hard fight, and Mylne's *Severn II* was often in the prize money among the eights. They were fine yachts, with all the elegance of the larger 12 Meters and with less expense and just as keen a racing season. Of all the International Rating Classes, the 8 Meter remains my favorite, and I feel it is a class which should be revived, with the original accommodation requirements enforced.

Besides the racers, large cruising yachts were also occasionally built by the Fifes in the 'thirties, such as the schooner *Altair*, launched in 1931. A 107-footer with 5938 square feet of sail in a classic gaff rig, and with a powerful auxiliary engine, *Altair* was amongst the larger yachts built at Fairlie. The yard also built some yachts which were then regarded as motorsailers by having a more powerful engine than usual and slightly less sail area than was common for their size. The 64' *Frea*, built in 1934, had the elegance of all the Fairlie yachts and a single-headsail Bermudian ketch rig with a "modest" sail area of 1622 square feet. In 1936, William and R. Balderston Fife designed and the Fairlie yard built the lovely cutter *Latifa* for Michael Mason, a 70-footer with a 52' waterline length, 15'3" beam and draft of 10'2". She was a most attractive cutter yacht, later rigged as a yawl, and the most interesting feature of her shapely hull was a well-formed canoe stern. One must assume that they were both responsible for this development, which was certainly more seaworthy than the usual counter and had been successfully used in many small cruising yachts for the previous 40 years. The next year the Fifes designed and built the beautiful 51' Bermudian sloop *Evenlode* for T. C. Ratsey of the celebrated sailmaking company. She was one of many yachts built just before and after

> After the war, the yard became the Fairlie Yacht Slip Company and continued to lay up and repair yachts of the smaller types, and its yachtbuilding tradition was carried on by the building of an occasional vessel.

World War II which conformed to the then-desirable 35' waterline length, with moderate overhangs which were encouraged by contemporary offshore rules. *Evenlode* was long a competitor in offshore events.

Late in 1938, William Fife and Son received an order to build the splendid 79' Bermudian yawl *Mariella* to the design of Alfred Mylne. She was launched in 1938, and in the two seasons before the war was one of the outstanding large cruisers in British waters. That spring the Fifes launched the auxiliary sloop *Merry Dancer*, another of the fast cruiser/handicap-racer/offshore-racer yachts of about the magic 35' waterline length at which the two designers were adept.

The Fairlie yard continued to build yachts "on spec" to the end. Their advertisement in Yachting World for September 1, 1939, two days before the outbreak of war, read: "Fast Bermudian rigged cruiser (now building) 35 ft. W.L. Suitable for ocean racing. Price and particulars on application." This yacht was completed in 1940, several months after war had begun, probably to clear the berth in the shed. After the war she was named *Solway Maid* and was sailed extensively in British, Scandinavian and continental European waters under the ownership of F. Ivan Carr. She was the last of the long and glorious line of yachts designed and built by the Fifes at Fairlie.

After the war, the yard became the Fairlie Yacht Slip Company under the management of Mr. Archie Macmillan, who had been many years with the firm. The yard continued to lay up and repair yachts of the smaller types favored by yachtsmen in postwar conditions, and its yachtbuilding tradition was carried on by the building of an occasional vessel, including *Tinto* for the 8 Meter International Cruiser/Racer class, now sadly defunct. This class was established on the Clyde in 1950, and boats were built for it until 1967 from designs by James McGruer (who conceived the rule), Arthur Robb and Morris and Lorimer. *Tinto* was designed by Archie Macmillan, and was unusual in the fleet in having a graceful canoe stern in the Fife tradition of the 1930s.

There were special qualities of integrity and grace to all the yachts which came out of Fairlie, from first to last. My own favorite among all the Fife yachts was the 90' yawl *Rendezvous*, designed and built in 1913 and later owned for cruising and for racing in the handicap class by Sir William Burton, a celebrated amateur helmsman who sailed Lipton's fourth *Shamrock* in the America's Cup challenge of 1920. For several years, my uncle, Captain Jim Barnard, was her skipper, and she laid up each winter in Rowhedge village, towering over the road when on marine railway, and displaying the grace and beauty of her Fife hull. Among her crew was Bill Woodward of Wivenhoe, for whom I produced my first motor fishing design. He recalled for me the way they raced her, telling me "However quick you was, you could never be too quick for your uncle..."

Rendezvous was a typical Fife-built yacht. The lovely sweep of her scrubbed deck planks melted into the varnished mahogany covering boards and the king plank, complemented by the dark varnished teak of the companion hatch and the skylights winking in the sun under the snow-white sail covers and above the spacious and comfortable cabins and saloon. In the long, tapering foc's'le with its vertical steel ladder and coal cooking stove, the rows of pipe cots were neatly lashed back above the long, grained locker tops. Uncle had a small cabin abreast the mainmast, where the bulkhead divided the crew from "the company" aft. Everything about *Rendezvous*, from the huge keelbolts to the truck of the main topmast head, was maintained like new, and her sails were set to perfection.

A magical vessel, and perhaps typical of the Fife genius. All of the yachtbuilding Fifes were remarkable men, and the vessels they built were as special to thousands of yachtsmen and professional hands as *Rendezvous* was to me. As Neil Munroe's Scottish "puffer" skipper Para Handy would have said: "Such agility! It was just sublime!"

BELLE AVENTURE

Described as "by any standard one of the world's most beautiful, flawlessly maintained yachts" by L.E. Nicholson in a recent WoodenBoat, *Belle Aventure* currently sails as a charter vessel out of Antigua, represented by the Nicholson charter organization in Nelson's Dockyard and, as noted, flawlessly maintained by Captain Paul Goss and his crew.

It was not always so. Designed and built by the Fifes in 1929 as a cruising ketch that sometimes raced on her home waters in Western Scotland, *Belle Aventure*, first named *Eileen,* was a pampered vessel until the mid-1950s. She was built for Louis V. Fulton, and sailed out of Greenock under Fulton and her second owner, Hugh MacLean, who renamed her *My Lady of Aros*. In 1938, she was acquired by Sir Alexander MacCormick and kept in Jersey as *Alison*. Charles E. Russell of Colchester owned her from 1947 to 1951, and in 1952 she became the yacht of Prince Omar Halim of Egypt as *Keyf.* She spent 20 years in the Med from the mid-1950s into the 1970s, allegedly made a voyage to the Far East in her old age, and was what one of her admirers describes as "a mess" by 1978 when she was bought by an English nobleman who prefers to keep his anonymity.

She was sailed back to the Clyde from Malta by a delivery crew and put into the yard of George McGruer at Clynder near Glasgow for a rebuilding and refitting under Lloyd's supervision that was so thorough the British yachting magazines found it extraordinary. Her construction by the men of Fairlie, with grown oak frames, galvanized steel floors, and 2″-thick teak planking, helped her keep her shape and her integrity during years of neglect, but it took two years of work in 1979-80 to bring her back. She was thoroughly refitted, with new wiring, plumbing, rigging and machinery, and it took hundreds of graving pieces to restore damage to her hull and deck work. Below decks, her walnut and maple saloon paneling was kept, and new teak-faced bulkheads were installed elsewhere. The saloon's gimballed dining table is the walnut original crafted by the Fairlie yard in 1929. As much original joinerwork as possible was kept and restored, including teak decklights and hatches worked like 18th-century furniture.

The reborn *Belle Aventure* was brought up to Lloyd's highest rating of 100 A1, and she was not modified for the charter trade. She carries only four guests on charters that in former years brought her to New England, and once to the Mediterranean, for the summer. In winter, she sails the Caribbean from a base in Antigua, and this year she will spend the summer in the islands. Her arrangement is the same as it was when she was built: chain locker in the forepeak, crew quarters for five forward with an adjacent head compartment, captain's cabin to starboard and galley to port forward of amidships, saloon amidships with dining table and upholstered settees, a two-berth guest cabin aft of amidships to starboard, and two head compartments, one serving the owner's stateroom, to port. The owner's cabin aft is spacious—indeed, grand—with a large double berth to starboard and a "library" to port.

A French yachting journalist has chosen several surviving Fife yachts for a forthcoming book on the 30 most beautiful yachts in the world, and *Belle Aventure* is one of them. As these few photos indicate, she's a proper choice. Yachts like this one were built in a time when beauty, integrity, good behavior and speed under sail were expected of great cruising yachts by their owners and by their builders. Money is certainly a factor in this equation, in 1984 as it was in 1929, but money is only an agent. Yachts like this are a magic synthesis of the dreams of owners, designers and builders.

Restored to the Lloyd's 100 A1 standard she knew at her launching in 1929, *Belle Aventure* sails on charter out of Antigua and makes occasional visits to cooler climes. Until this summer, she competed in the Classic Yacht Regatta during the Labor Day weekend in Newport, where these photos were taken. Although she was described by one of her admirers as "a mess" in 1978 when she was acquired by her present owner, she spent two years in the McGruer yard in Scotland and came out looking as glorious as she does here. She's an especially good example of the fine points of Fife workmanship. The saloon, a corner of which is shown below, is paneled in walnut and maple, and the joinerwork is richly beaded and detailed. Even the decklight at right has this quality of fine workmanship in first-quality teak. For good reason, *Belle Aventure* is considered one of the world's most beautiful yachts.

LOA: 95'
LOD: 84'6"
LWL: 60'5"
Beam: 17'7"
Draft: 10'7"
Sail Area: 3000 sq. ft.
Ballast: 28 tons
Displacement: N.A.
Fuel: 500 gallons
Water: 500 gallons
Power: G.M. 4-71 diesel
Designer: W. and R. B. Fife
Builder: William Fife & Son, Fairlie, Scotland

NAUTICAL QUARTERLY

ALTAIR

One of the last large yachts designed and built by the Fifes, *Altair* was launched in 1931 with scantlings and specifications in excess of Lloyd's' highest rating of 100 A1. She was built for Captain Guy H. MacCaw of Scotland, for what her original prospectus describes as "a contemplated maiden voyage to the South Sea Islands," and she passed through two other British owners during the 1930s. In 1949 she arrived in Spain and passed through four owners before being acquired in 1972 by Miguel Sans Mora.

Captain Sans Mora, the oldest licensed Master in Spain, sails her with his family and a professional crew out of the Royal Yacht Club in Barcelona, and in August and September every year she makes a long cruise eastward to French and Italian ports. This is yachting in the old style and on a grand scale, in a vessel that has thankfully been kept much as she was at her launching.

Altair's planking is 2½"-thick Indonesian teak on 5" x 7" oak frames, and her bottom is sheathed in copper, as it was in 1931 when she was ready for the South Seas. Below decks forward are crew accommodations for eight, along with a two-berth captain's cabin and crew's dayroom and galley. A large saloon with dining table and electric fireplace is amidships, and there are five cabins for the owner's party aft. Much of her below-decks paneling is walnut. *Altair* has kept her original name as well as her original Lloyds classification of 100 A1, and this last is evidence of the quality of her ownership over more than 50 years. She has been given a new spruce deck in recent years, along with new sails and such modern gear as electric winches for handling her 5938 square feet of sail.

Altair sails today as a tribute to the design genius of William and R. Balderston Fife, to the skills of her Scottish builders, and to the love and care lavished on her by a succession of owners.

NAUTICAL QUARTERLY

A grand old schooner built by the Fifes in 1931, *Altair* has been kept by a succession of owners much as she was when she was launched. She is owned now by Captain Miguel Sans Mora of Spain, and she sails out of the Royal Yacht Club of Barcelona on family cruises that normally include visits to French and Italian ports every August and September.

Some of her sumptuous spaces are shown here: details of guest staterooms above and below, the saloon with its electric fireplace above left, and the navigator's space in the forward part of the deckhouse.

LOA: 107′8″
LWL: 77′9″
Beam: 20′5″
Draft: 13′2″
Sail Area: 5938 sq. ft.
Ballast: 80 tons
Displacement: N.A.
Fuel: 3000 liters
Water: 4½ tons
Power: 286-hp Baudouin diesel
Designer: W. and R. B. Fife
Builder: William Fife & Son, Fairlie, Scotland

COTTON BLOSSOM IV

When Walter Wheeler discovered *Maikai II*, soon to be *Cotton Blossom IV*, his previous *Cotton Blossom*, U.S.12 #1, had been destroyed by fire shortly before. He found *Maikai* in a yard in Fairhaven, where she had been laid up during World War II, and the story goes that he had reservations about her only because of her low headroom. He came back to the shed after a few minutes of reflection, pulled open her cabin sole, and decided that the framing would permit the sole to be dropped three inches. Wheeler bought her, had her refitted and rerigged as a yawl with the counsel of Bill Luders, and brought her into the Class A lists of ocean racing in 1952.

Built by the Fifes in 1925-26 and launched as the Marconi-rigged cutter *Hallowe'en*, this yacht had made her mark in ocean racing from the beginning, finishing the 1926 Fastnet Race third on corrected time and setting an elapsed-time record for the old Fastnet course that still stands. She was based on a 15-meter design, but was structurally much heavier, and she is alleged to be the first yacht designed specifically for the new sport of ocean racing. She was the first Marconi-rigged yacht to race offshore.

Her owner, Colonel J. F. N. Baxendale, quit while he was ahead, rerigged her with a gaff-headed main, and cruised her in the Med for several seasons. Sold to Norway, she became *Magda XII*, flagship of the Royal Norwegian Yacht Club. In the later 1930s, she was bought by an American, John B. Mickles, and cruised New England from a base in Marblehead until World War II. As *Cotton Blossom IV*, campaigned by Walter Wheeler, his family and friends, she competed in six Bermuda Races, more than a dozen New York Yacht Club Cruises, and many Annapolis-Newport contests.

When Walter Wheeler retired from business, *Cotton Blossom IV* became a cruising boat again, and she would shortly begin a new career as a charter vessel. In the summer of 1970, she was acquired by two young sailors, Neil Guertin and Charles Gee, who had admired her for years. She sailed the Caribbean in winter and New England in summer until 1974. Currently owned by Dr. Bruce and Judith Eissner of Marblehead, she does some summer charter work in New England, as well as PHRF racing in Massachusetts Bay, and she joins other *grandes dames*, including *Belle Aventure*, every Labor Day weekend in Newport for the Classic Yacht Regatta.

Cotton Blossom IV is another tribute to loving ownership and to skillful design and construction in first-quality teak and oak. When she was wooded in 1974, only two soft spots were found in her teak planking after 48 years.

On this page, a few details of *Cotton Blossom*'s restored interior. Her paneling and joinerwork were recently refinished ashore—with 11 coats of varnish—then put back aboard.

LOA: 71'6"
LWL: 49'11"
Beam: 14'6"
Draft: 9'6"
Sail Area: 2400 sq. ft.
Ballast: N.A.
Displacement: 78,600 pounds
Fuel: 85 gallons
Water: 500 gallons
Power: 85-hp Perkins diesel
Designer: W. and R. B. Fife
Builder: William Fife & Son, Fairlie, Scotland

CORRESPONDENCE

Dear Editor:

It appears that nearly every letter to NQ is effusive in its praise for the publication. Witness the first letter in issue 25. It begins, "The August issue was stunning as always." Perhaps that is the only way to begin a letter to NQ if one wants it to be published.

Regardless, my letter does not begin that way and it is not about letters. It is about Len Pearce's painting in NQ25 on page 30 entitled, "The Cutter Yachts Off the Isle of Wight." The accompanying narrative quotes Mr. Pearce as saying that he has "done a little sailing, but not very much." Maybe his lack of nautical acumen can, therefore, be excused. In the above referenced painting, only one of the four primary yachts' heading, sail trim, and angle of heel bear any reference to the direction of the wind.

Let's keep a weather eye on any painting of a nautical subject matter reproduced in future issues.
William Baker
Annapolis, Maryland

Editor's Note: The actual title of that painting is "Beginner's Class In The Cutter Yachts Off The Isle of Wight." The sail-trim lesson occurred the following week.

Dear Editor:

I enjoyed the excellent article about Don Shead in NQ26; over the years we have been both teammates and competitors but always good friends. I am happy to have had a small hand in getting him started in the design business at which he has been so successful.

Two small points for the record: As stated, Don, Tommy Sopwith and I took three identical Wynne-Walters 17-foot boats to the Paris 6-hour race in 1962. These were the Volvo-Penta powered *Wyn-Mill* deep-vee design which I had raced successfully in various U.S. marathon events; Don had the idea that they would be ideal for the incredible chop generated by the boat wakes and vertical banks of the Seine in this race. Tommy led the race for a period before a broken engine mount pierced a hole in the oil pan and Don suffered the same fate. However, contrary to the statement that none of us placed, I actually won the R-I inboard class, was second overall and received the Index of Performance Trophy, which was presented in the name of Monsieur le President, Charles de Gaulle. The experience of racing as part of the Shead-Sopwith team, which included cruising up the Seine on *Philante V* carrying Tommy's race boat, are among my favorite memories.

Another minor point which I realize could not be covered in the article is that Walters and I designed and drove the first aluminum offshore race boat (Maritime, 1965) which won several U.S. races and the Viareggio-Bastia race. A second boat of this design (Thunderbird, 1966) was powered with twin Pratt & Whitney 550 horsepower gas turbines. It won its first race, the Sam Griffith Memorial, and was immediately ruled out of further competition. I know exactly how Don and Tommy felt about their hassles over gas-turbine rules.

Finally, I would like to emphasize that Tommy Sopwith really won the Offshore World Championship in 1970; only a ridiculous technical ruling by Red Crise, who thrived on such publicity, robbed him of the Sam Griffith Memorial Trophy.
James R. Wynne
Wynne Marine, Inc.
Miami, Florida

Dear Editor:

We launched the big skiff the other day, the one we've been restoring all winter. It was an Event. You should have been there. Everyone else was, including Coots O'Neal, the original builder. He came over from Boothbay Harbor. It was the first time he had been east of Edgecomb, so E. H. Morgan showed him around town. That was a big mistake. Coots had a beer at Gonagle's Sheet Metal Shop, a shot of Old Overholt at the Farmer's Union, another beer at Hansen's Fuel & Ice, a six-pack on the porch of Bannock's General Store, and who-knows-whatall in the back of Morgan's Hudson Hornet down at the Town Landing. Come launching time, Coots and E. H. had just about forgot what we had gathered for. Coots was to give the launching speech but he was confused and thought we were going to bury the boat. It was a rousing oration—all about the glories of the boatbuilding wars and we'll never see the likes of these boats again and damn the IOR and it's a shame we have to bury this boat and why don't we burn her for her fastenings at least and does anyone in the crowd here have a match and how about a little gasoline to soak down the garboards and... Well, you guessed it. Before anyone could stop him E. H. emptied a can of gas in the boat and Coots tossed a match into the thing. There was a whump, then a pillar of flame and a lot of black smoke. Morgan was just terrible. He was weaving around the launching ramp with a bottle of Pusser's rum cheering Coots on: "Attaboy, Coots. We need those fastenings." Luckily the Volunteer Fire Department was on maneuvers and got right over here to put out the fire before it could do little more than burn the paint off her. The skiff's out in the harbor right now, looking a mite ragged, but afloat at least. Like I said, you should have been there.
Fred Brooks
Bucksport, Maine

Dear Editor:

I was interested in NQ25 with the article on Ray Hunt and the International 110. Fleet 16 is one of the oldest fleets in the International 110 Yacht Racing Association, dating to 1940. I have owned and raced #370 since the early '50s. It was a pleasant surprise to discover the article, as we are generating new interest in 110s and it will help in our efforts. We may be the only fleet which owns its own 'glass hull molds.
Allan M. Phillips
Honolulu, Hawaii

Dear Editor:

Not only did your two Ray Hunt related articles (NQ22 and NQ25) maintain the superior quality for which I have invested in this magnificent quarterly, but they also spoke eloquently of the Yankee genius of the subject and, as all good writing does, reminded the reader of those ideas and events where subject's and reader's courses have crossed tacks.

I first knew of Ray Hunt from my father who grew up a few years behind him in Duxbury and from the boats we rented from him at the Town Landing in Marblehead, a short walk from my family's house there. That office was closed in the early 1950s and the boats and other assets transferred to Otie Milmore who ran the Marblehead Rental Boat Company for 25 years thereafter. When I wasn't spending my summer hours working for Otie maintaining Hunt-designed boats he rented, I was a paid hand on two lovely Hunt-designed Concordia yawls or I was racing my own 110 on weekends.

There was nothing obscure about Ray Hunt to a young sailor growing up in Marblehead in the '50s and '60s. Ray had a special meaning to many of us because he was so often present. Like the equally gifted L. Francis Herreshoff, Ray Hunt tinkered with his designs before our very eyes. We occasionally saw him running around the harbor in a varnished Hickman sea sled (a forerunner of the Boston Whaler) or testing a keel-centerboard version of the 210's bulb keel. The exterior bottom stringers so familiar on today's Bertrams first appeared on *Yonder* just before *Moppie* was conceived. Because so many of Hunt's designs were given life at Graves Yacht Yard, we frequently observed him overseeing construction there. Over the years we were able to watch *Quixotic*, *Easterner* and *Minotaur* take shape in Marblehead yards and train and tune in Marblehead waters. The deck of his banana-colored catamaran is even reputed to have provided a romantic interlude for an occasional nautical date.

My greatest thrill came when *Minotaur's* owner, John Mooney, at the behest of Otie Milmore, invited me to crew for the 1960 Olympic trials. *Minotaur* had just been launched from Graves yard and Ray was helping John tune her. I learned early that Ray sailed by feel more than anything else. I can still see him, arm resting on *Minotaur's* after deck with her tiller gently suspended between his parallel thumb and index finger, feeling her not just with his fingers, but with his whole body as well. *Minotaur's* jumpers led inside the mast above the spreaders and outside the mast to turnbuckles above the mast step. Sensing some imperfection in the rig, Hunt asked Mooney to tighten the starboard spreader one-half a turn. Within a moment of completion, he told us convincingly that he actually felt a difference!

Evidence of his influence is everywhere, but it is difficult today to find a sailor/architect who combines so many of Ray Hunt's qualities and talents.
Mark W. Kellogg
Severna Park, Maryland

Dear Editor:

I have just spent the last few hours with NQ26 and enjoyed it as usual, but something makes me wish to write. Starting at the back I look at the story on Don Shead and wonder why he looks a lot older than I, in view of being born a dozen years behind me. I am also often surprised at my Rotary fellow members looking older, being younger, and if anyone says it is because of a hard life I can only point to the fact I had 77 holes in me being wounded three times

CORRESPONDENCE

before I was nineteen during WWII.

Anyway, after almost hitting a granite dock during an outboard race in 1936 as driver for Johnson/Finland, I have not until very recently been interested in fast boats, even though I worked with John Hacker for eight years from 1952 to 1960, until his death. Now I'm up to my ears in fast (and slow) boats.

Leafing back through nostalgia of "real yachts," such as those of the late 1920s, I recall I had the *Delphine* for sale and had Walt Disney in Grosse Pointe to look at it as a possible "floating Disneyland." It was for sale for $500,000; Mr. Disney offered $400,000 and I was dreaming of a 7% commission ($28,000). We found Mrs. Horace Dodge cruising on a 57' Norwegian motorsailer from Nordkapp (North Cape) to Spitsbergen (Svalbard), and she told Walt Disney to pay $500,000 or "go to hell," while aboard that small boat. I think she was then 83 years old or close to it. Was not the *Delphine* one of this fleet of gracious yachts of the 1920s?

Next comes *Pardon Me*, which I saw when it was *Lockpat III*, and naturally my admiration for John L. Hacker clouds any but good comments. He was such a gentle non-businessman with such fantastic talent, officially a vegetarian, but many times seen in non-frequented cafeterias (low-priced) gorging himself on hamburgers, french fries and chocolate cakes. I did meet and didn't like Pat Locke one ounce.

Then looking at *Boomerang* brings to mind a small 19' sloop, the Swift 19, I designed some 15-16 years ago. It was very fast, but only one was built. Then two years ago, I designed a 22'6" version, and an aluminum boat of this design two weeks ago literally clobbered a fleet in Newport, Oregon. This has prompted a local Tacoma man to want a 23'9" version to be known as the Courier 24, but that is not why I write this down. I do it because essentially the Swift 19 and the *Boomerang* have similar looks and I just wonder if I should have expanded long ago and now be in league with Frers and other Maxi designers? But I don't think so, as I don't think I'd get along famously with the customers in that class.

The Dinosaurs of Sail do not interest or bother me as I'm not much for nostalgia, but I definitely think I can compete with Frers on boats like *Volador* (I know only a few millionaires, none interested in boats, except Malcolm Forbes, and he has one.)

Speaking of him, I must tell you that he invited a very ragged sailor party aboard the *Highlander* during a cold, blustery, rainy evening at the 79th Street Marina in September, 1954. We were four couples taking a 54' imported Norwegian sloop from New York to Detroit via the Hudson River, the N.Y. Barge Canal, Buffalo, Lake Erie, and the Detroit River. That trip is a fine story by itself, close to fiction, to be told.

Anyway, in 1979 I found the log of that trip, read about Forbes' invitation and wondered if anyone ever sent him a thank-you note, which I then did. I guess he liked a 25-year-old thank-you better than a new one because he said in a return note something to the effect that an immediate thank-you would be just that; one 25 years later was special.

So, moving backwards we come to Huisman. After reading about his yard, he is about the only builder I *really* would like to know because I agree with him that tradition can be very dangerous in a world full of new ways. About 25 years ago I invented a machine which would produce wooden frames to the exact shapes and bevels for all stations and frames, but then tupperware took over. Now, however, after all these years, there is interest in it and I'm slowly drawing it for making it and I have an awful lot of interest because of the growing wood-boat building interest and the new technologies in building wooden boats. My machine will eliminate lofting and making of frames and you can readily see what this means. Yes, Huisman is okay —new things, new ways, new materials.

Seascapes. I have seen too many really beautiful ones to get excited about some in a book. The PTs also leave me a bit cold. Didn't Sutphen build a bunch of them in Canada in 1940-41 when there was an outcry about building for England in the U.S.?

Robby Naish makes me wish I was as smart as I am but 40 years younger, at least...and that brings me to the beginning of NQ26 after yet another enjoyable few hours.
Nils Lucander, N.A.
Speed at Sea Designs
Tacoma, Washington

Editor's Note: It is always a pleasure to hear from Nils Lucander, the versatile (and voluble) Finnish-born designer of everything from daysailers to motor yachts to large fishboats, as well as ingenious marine devices. He provides more information above than questions; but, to try to answer the questions: Yes, Mrs. Horace E. Dodge's "big" *Delphine* was one of the super motor yachts of the 1920s. Built in 1921 by the Great Lakes Engineering Works, she was 257'8" overall, and appropriately palatial. The "small" *Delphine*, her predecessor, was 187'8". As to the rumored Canadian-built PTs for Britain, we find no evidence that Henry Sutphen (Elco) built any of them, although there were some patrol boats built in Canada. Minette-Shields built Motor Torpedo Boats (MTBs) for Britain, to designs by Doug Van Patten; a few of the Vosper designs were built at Canadian yards during the war; and Canadian Powerboat turned out some of the 77' PTs.

Dear Editor:

My NQ back-issue order arrived this weekend. Magnificent! It is quite an impressive gathering of superb books/magazines. After reading a few of the back issues, we gathered up our gear and spent the weekend sailing about the bay and the Gulf in my Hunter 54. Your publication is an inspiration, to say the least. My thanks for the most beautiful boat book in the world. I even enjoy the "stink-pot" coverage, which is rare for a rag-man.
John Hunter Todd
Houston, Texas

Dear Editor:

We in the University of Connecticut Sailing Club are building a fine tradition of competitive and recreational sailing. Our club is nearly twenty years old. We have been sailing on Coventry Lake for recreational purposes and at many other sites during races. Our fleet of six Penguins, three Lasers and five Fireballs has been serving us well, but we've run into a few problems.

We have a Boston Whaler that we use as a rescue craft. It is very handy for plucking submerged Penguins and wet sailors from the water, as well as for keeping an eye on neophyte sailors going in all directions at any given moment. This past December, the motor was stolen from our Whaler and it's going to cost plenty to replace it. We haven't the funds to even begin to cover such costs. We're asking for donations of any amount to help us get the Whaler back in operation. It's paradoxical, but a cogent reality that we need to have the powerboat in operation in order to continue teaching basic sailing. If you've ever pitch-poled a Penguin, you can appreciate what I'm saying. They're not unlike large bathtubs—only heavier.

Donations of supplies, materials, and sundries will also be considered by the club. If you'd like more information from us, please feel free to write or call:
Bill Collins, Yeoman
UConn Sailing Club
Box U-8
Storrs, Connecticut 06268
(203) 742-6160
Bill Collins
Storrs, Connecticut

Dear Editor:

What a super article on Grand Craft in NQ25. The layout, color, technical section, logo usage and total concept is just outstanding! The whole gang at Grand Craft is very proud to be featured in what we consider to be the finest boating publication available. We all thank you many times as the books will become family mementos for ourselves and our craftsmen.

Everyone who sees the magazine wants to know how to obtain one. I feel that the 25th issue was certainly one of the best yet because of the diversity of all the articles. Keep it up!

I also think the advertising was very tasteful and actually an addition. There was no detraction from quality whatsoever. I, too, feel it is wise not to advertise boats or marine-related items
Steve Northuis
Grand Craft Corp.
Holland, Michigan

CREDITS

Cover:	Benjamin Mendlowitz
1:	John E. Hutton, Jr., M.D.
3-13:	Chuck Place
14-19:	Michael Levitt
20 & 21:	Courtesy of the New York Yacht Club Library
22 & 23:	Courtesy of the Museum of the City of New York
24:	Print by William Foster, London, 1867, from a private collection, photographed by Ashley Studios
28-35:	Paintings by the artist, Norma Jay, photographed by MPS Photographic Services, Inc., Costa Mesa, CA
36 & 37:	Courtesy of Huckins Yacht Corp.
38:	Stanley Rosenfeld, top, Courtesy of Huckins Yacht Corp., bottom
42:	Morris Rosenfeld, top left, middle center, and lower left and right; courtesy of Huckins Yacht Corp., top center and right, middle left; Norman Fortier, middle right; Loyd Sandgren, lower center
45:	Courtesy of Huckins Yacht Corp.
46-48:	Morris Rosenfeld
49-53:	Stanley Rosenfeld
54 & 55:	Chuck Place
56 & 57:	Wally Rediske
58:	Wally Rediske, top and bottom right; Chuck Place, bottom left
65:	Chuck Place
66-69:	John E. Hutton, Jr., M.D.
72:	Courtesy of the U.S. Naval Academy Museum
73:	Courtesy of the Archives, U.S. Naval Academy
74:	John DeGast
78:	Courtesy of the U.S. Naval Academy Museum
80 & 81:	John E. Hutton, Jr., M.D.
82:	Mark Newman/Tom Stack & Associates
83:	Gary Randall/Tom Stack & Associates
84 & 85:	Robert W. Hernandez, National Audubon Society Collection/PR
87:	Robert W. Hernandez, National Audubon Society Collection/PR
88:	Leonard Lee Rue II, National Audubon Society Collection/PR
91-93:	Paintings by Richard Ellis
94-99:	Photographs by Daniel Allisy/Sea and See, line drawings courtesy of Henri Wauquiez et Cie
102-119:	Benjamin Mendlowitz
121:	Photograph of Fred Brooks as a child, courtesy of the Wood Neck Marine Antiques Exchange.

Pages 94-99 commissioned by Henri Wauquiez et Cie, all by arrangement with Fraser Fraser-Harris, yacht surveyor.

Nautical Quarterly is printed by Federated Lithographers, Inc., Providence, Rhode Island, and bound by The Book Press, Inc., Brattleboro, Vermont.